Advance Praise

"Kevin McGary's latest book, *Freed to be Servant and Slave*, is perhaps the most significant book I have read in the past decade. Maybe three decades. It is *must* reading for all who call themselves "Christian," from the back row pew to the pulpit. This book has the potential to change the course of history, and I am not prone to exaggerate! ~Christian Overman

Dr. Christian Overman is the founding director of Worldview Matters. An international speaker, Dr. Overman has taught on the topic of biblical worldview throughout the United States, as well as in Central America, Europe, Asia and Africa.

FREED TO BE SERVANT AND SLAVE...

Finally breaking free of ALL bondage
as a "new creation"...IN CHRIST!

Kevin McGary

RATIONAL FREE PRESS
Toronto. San Jose. Boise

Contact the author at: KevinMcGary@RationalFreePress.com

Published in Canada and the United States by Rational Free Press Other titles by this author: "DEI IN 3D" "Woked Up! *Finally Putting An Ax To the Taproot Of White Supremacy and Racism in America*" "The War on Women From The Root To The Fruit!" "JUST Justly Justice"

ISBN: 978-1-77772018-9-0

Relational Publishing

Table of Contents

Dedication

This book is dedicated to two remarkable individuals who have recently departed, yet their impact remains enduring. Larry D. Wiens, a remarkable businessman, marketplace leader, and devoted family man, consistently exhibited the fruits of the Spirit and unwavering commitment to the Lord and His Kingdom. Larry's life serves as an inspirational legacy, touching countless others who were profoundly influenced by his joyful embrace of being a servant and slave to Jesus.

Dean Nelson was a valiant warrior for God, dedicating every aspect of his life under the Lordship of Christ. Despite being several years my junior, he became my leader and mentor, and I can only hope to approach the completion of my work in this realm with the same dedication he exemplified. Dean, a "Kingdom first" marketplace leader, emitted the sweet fragrance of the fruits of the Spirit throughout his life. His legacy endures through his incredible wife, children, and close friends. We will forever cherish his contribution to our lives and the world.

These remarkable men served as inspiration for me to pen this book, delving deeper into the realm of what it truly means to be a servant and slave to Christ.

Author's note

This book can lead you through a spiritual journey to the depths of your soul. It is designed to help confirm whether you are currently living to God's highest and best standard as slave to Jesus, or living beneath the standards God established. Most will discover we are living well beneath God's design. If you're not living life according to the God-ordained standard, this book help you thoroughly understand the severity of the need to, and also, the consequences for not.

We agree this book has a peculiar title. It purposely and strategically presents a perplexing paradox intertwined with seemingly competing dichotomies. This is not done merely to be coy or clever; it is done to present a dormant truth that has been ignored or forgotten.

There are many notions that may come to mind with this book title, but in particular, two possibilities should immediately come to mind. First, "Free to be a Servant and Slave" connotes that one can be "set free" yet choose to go back into bondage and become a "servant" and "slave." The second meaning could be that one is actually set free by becoming a servant and slave; *freedom by becoming a servant and slave.* Neither of these notions is comforting to the soul. To our "natural mind" (with preconceived notions about these distinctions), these notions appear unnatural and perplexing when contemplating the horrors of being bound as a servant or an enslaved person.

How can anyone surmise that yielding to becoming a servant, or even worse, a slave is the ideal condition to set one free (physically, or in the mind, soul and spirit)? Attempting to wrap the mind around these arcane concepts can make one's brain hurt, but putting our brain to work on this apparent conundrum is a worthy and life-changing exercise. (Note: this book does not excuse, or in any way, trivialize or condone coerced human slavery whereby people are maltreated, maligned and abused. Such forms of slavery should always be condemned and viewed as inhumane and contemptible)

There is a state of being whereby the human soul feels it is experiencing "real" freedom. This freedom is experienced when principled foundations of truth are fully exposed and understood. Truth is such a powerful force it breaks chains and bounds. Remember, the Word of God declares, "...you will know the truth, and the truth will set (or make) you free." (Jn 8:32)

As God prepares warriors in His remanent armies for this season of Kingdom conquest and breakthroughs, breaking the bonds and chains that grip humanity is vital. Therefore, this book's promise is to break chains that have previously prevented experiencing real freedom due to bonds (literal or mental) that restrict and inhibit human flourishing. Due to the intensity of the subject and the claims of newfound freedoms lying herein, I anticipate you will find this book compelling, convicting, and even life-saving.

Freed To be Servant and Slave presents a fresh journey… your release from bondage and a renewed freedom awaits!

Special note: At the risk of grammatical incorrectness, throughout this book, "satan" is intentionally portrayed in lowercase. He is lowly, loathsome, and a definitive loser; satan doesn't merit or deserve any dignities, so this book purposely casts him in the proper context.

Introduction

"FREEDOM!"

The ubiquitous cry within every heart is to be free. A basic human desire is to experience life as unencumbered and untethered from any restrictive bounds that create barriers preventing experiencing life's boundless flourishing. But achieving freedom is the exception, not the rule. Why? Why, even in the face of significant human progression (including vast innovations and world wealth), are there large populations of humanity enduring various forms of bondage?

Vast history documents the horrors of people being bound and enslaved globally. Slavery has occurred since human inception, and no region on the planet has escaped it. That said, it is easy to comprehend why the fundamentals and tenets of slavery are met with extreme contempt; torture and bondage restrict the innate human cry and demand for freedom.

The need to be set free, whether from physical chains or in the recesses of the heart, mind, and soul, is universal. With the ubiquitous cry for freedom overlying every race, gender, tribe, and region, why does it seem that humankind has not progressed much further toward freedom? It seems humanity gets progressively worse with each passing generation. Suicide deaths have skyrocketed globally. It is hard to fathom, but considering the amount of human suffering, it seems the entire globe is under a cloud of oppression and bondage. Certainly wars, rumors of war and various active slave trade (including global human and sex trafficking) operations occurring in sizeable regions of the world, increase the desire for human flourishing and freedom. Outside of the horrors and abuse of physical enslavement, oppression and bondage has moved beyond physical abuses and into mainstream thinking as a pervasive notion in culture. Many can only imagine the horrors of actual physical enslavement, nevertheless say they feel similar suffering due to an overwhelming sense of bondage and oppression. Virtue signaling about being a victim of bondage and oppression is now mainstreamed.

In our current cultural context, some examples of bondage appear as suffering with overwhelming feelings of loneliness, uncontrollable bouts of rage/hate and addictions, enduring constant "breakdowns" (unpredictable interruptions in the "flow of life") and loss, and persistent chaos. Most people can thus grasp the intense trials and suffering of Job in the Bible. Many feel they can relate to Job's life. The book of Job explores what happens during times of intense suffering. The story confirms Job was a righteous man, yet he undergoes immense personal suffering and loss. In the end, it confirms that

God did not produce Job's suffering; he was not under God's wrath. Conversely, even with the incredible personal losses and suffering, Job was protected under God's mercy since God would not allow satan to take his life. The story of Job confirms the "god of this world," satan, must ask permission from Yahweh ("God most high") to access humanity and produce acts that steal, kill and destroy. In this realm, satan is quite limited! But, as the progenitor of all suffering and wrath, satan (alone) is responsible for all human suffering and oppression. And it is God alone who provides new mercies and the strength for humanity to endure.

Satan's realm is replete with myriad dysfunctions and chaos purposely designed to produce boundless suffering and bondage. Feelings of loneliness, fear, depression and innumerable other issues (like racism, nihilism, sexism, secularism, denominationalism, etc.) dominating culture have generated a cultural mood of helplessness and hopelessness similar to the life and trials of Job. Job contended with these issues as his suffering culminated in feeling all alone and (at some level) betrayed. In the end, Job realized he was not a victim, he was a victor. He was not alone; God was with him and protecting him in the midst of extreme darkness and difficulty. The truth is, Job's experiences were extraordinary, but many people today feel they can relate. At this point in human history, many feel victimized by "the world."

It has become a global theme to label oneself as a victim who is "set upon" and perpetually oppressed by various bondages that arise out of loneliness and chaos (like racism, sexism, "colonialism," etc.). Neglecting the various forms of physical slavery occurring globally, culture seems now to dictate that every malady of the human condition is to be blamed on bondage to some kind of oppression or oppressive scheme. Human enslavement and suffering now goes beyond levels of abuse due to physical pain, and now encompasses mental anguish/pain and its impact on the mind, body and spirit.

Existing cultural paradigms seem to elevate suffering in the mind as a pervasive norm. Everyone seems to suffer from *bondage to* and *oppression by* something! With human suffering now "mainstreamed" as a trait fundamental to the human condition, the pursuit of freedom (truly being set free) is paramount.

"Freed to Be Servant and Slave" aims to deliver freedom! It intends to provide a more grounded analysis and solutions for being set free and experiencing real freedom. This book delivers a fuller vision of freedom by providing a comprehensive perspective on God-given expressions of what it means to be truly free.

It must be noted that, by definition, freedom is literally impossible without God (our Creator and Master). As you read, challenge yourself with this fact, *God is the only answer*, as a backdrop to your assumptions and prevailing thoughts. In the end, I am sure you will conclude along with me that God is the only answer to the cultural tide now harvesting an endless bounty of bondage and oppression.

Again, the short answer is, God is the only answer; He ends enslavement and suffering by delivering freedom and abundance!

Let's get freed!

One

"We have fallen and can't get up!"

Remember the commercials about someone who has fallen down and is incapable of getting up? We might joke about the commercial, but it confirmed that serious consequences, including loss of life, can occur for people (mostly elderly and impaired) who can't timely get outside help in the effort to arise. Technology now allows impaired people to be "set free" by knowing immediate outside help can be accessed anytime if/when needed. Instead of being immobilized by the fear of falling and not having help, fear and helplessness is now mitigated and replaced with confidence and newfound freedom. Ironically, that commercial provides a good analogy to the plight of humanity.

Because of Adam and Eve's rebellion in the Garden of Eden, humanity is in a "fallen" state and also needs "outside help" to arise. Rebellion set up the baseline plight of humanity, as now everyone is born into a fallen state. The fallen state of humanity culminates with death, destruction, chaos, and, most pervasively, bondage and oppression (either physical or in the mind) that is inescapable. Issues plaguing humanity require outside help. Since the great "I AM," Yahweh is our creator who sits outside our realm, He is the only one who can help. We cannot resolve issues plaguing humanity in our own strength, so we (like the analogy of the elderly and infirmed) who fall and can't get up are immobilized by fear and bondage. "We've fallen and can't get up." Our only help and hope come from the God who created the heavens and the earth, the Most High God of the Bible. Only God, our creator, will set us free.

The world is "Jobified." Incessant cries from those who find themselves being tormented by cultural trends that point to bondage and myriad forms of oppression is overwhelming. Unfortunately, bondage and oppression have become the defining cultural phenomenon. This phenomenon is not limited to geographical regions; it's global. Irrespective of traditions, cultural settings, or communities, these days, it seems no individual is out of reach of feeling debilitated and in bondage due to some level of (perceived or literal) oppression. This is quite problematic because immobilizing and destabilizing forms of bondage and oppression are the antithesis of freedom. Said differently, people worldwide suffer more now than ever before due to what can be distilled down to emotions of not being free (seemingly demanded by cultural trends). Overwhelmed with the emotions of being fearful, offended, enslaved, and oppressed, people find solace in culture (knowing that countless others suffer the same) but find no actual relief within cultural trends. Instead, culture perpetuates and agitates aggrievement, which only exacerbates the trend. Many recent articles about depression and suicide confirm these trends are at record high levels globally.[1] Why have these trends soared?

The fallen world is part of a cosmic battle. The fight is driven by a fallen power intent on destroying humanity. And without having a say or choice in the matter, humanity is born and fully enlisted into this cosmic battle being waged in spiritual realms that have raged since the beginning of time. Notably, chaos and bondage are the primary instruments and fundamental attributes that our foe, "the god of this world," uses with the intent to perpetually enslave.

The fall of man in the Garden of Eden marked the beginning of the unleashing of our nemesis' ability to actively interfere with and undermine humanity. 2 Corinthians 4:4 confirms, "satan, who is the god of this world, has blinded the minds of those who don't believe..." The god of this world has fervent hate and disdain for Yahweh/God and His entire creation; the torment of humanity in all its forms comes from our foe (satan). Notably, he designs all instruments of bondage and despair in order to cause fear and immobilization. When we are immobilized, we are stuck in a state of suffering and constrained into bondage. The cosmic battle humanity is born into automatically (by default) overlays a fallen state producing bondage, not freedom. Freedom is not part of satan's schemes, but bondage and oppression are; therefore, the world system (including culture and secular traditions) is specifically inclined toward satan's vision. The good news is that the god of this world can be overcome, and humanity can be freed. But only our creator, Yahweh/God, provides the necessary interventions for mankind's freedom.

WELCOME TO THE MATRIX

Persistent levels of bondage and oppression plague mankind (seemingly unabated) because we are blinded (by our foe satan) and have not realized the specific pathway that God intended for humanity. As the cosmic battle between "good"/God and "evil"/satan rages around us, most are blind to the battle, and therefore, the pathway to freedom is obscured. While unseen, the specter that is constantly unfolding is epic. Ironically, humanity seems to be caught in similar parallels observed in the movie "The Matrix." Similar to the Matrix movie, there is a constant struggle in the battle between evil (represented in the movie as the machines) and humans (people pursuing good and truth).

The Matrix movie is cast in dark shadows (indicative of the strength of evil), and a stark picture of the cosmic battle between good and evil, light and darkness emerges. The Neo character was the "chosen one" in the movie and was destined to liberate humanity from the elusive world of the matrix – likewise, we have "The One" (Yeshua/Jesus), who is our chosen Savior destined to free humanity.

The Matrix itself can be directly compared to the deceptive nature of illusionary world systems, and likewise, humanity lives in an illusion created by our foe. The illusions we grapple with are false narratives designed to entrap, ensnare, and enslave us. Fundamentally (as depicted in The Matrix), we live in false realities within a world system that we believe to be true, but they are concocted by our foe (the god of this world); they are purposely designed as worldly illusions and distractions. Another similarity in the movie is that humans there have the power to choose their path and determine their destiny (by either taking the "red pill" or choosing to remain blinded to reality). This is the exact parallel for mankind; we can choose our pathway and destiny! We have approached a time for being "red-pilled." This is a time for choosing!

The pathway to freedom that Yahweh/God designed is not made up of complicated formulas or processes. It is based on following the pattern of Yeshua (Jesus). God sent His Son as our perfect example to help us understand how to "live, move, and have our being" (Acts 17:28) in this realm. With Yeshua as our perfect example, we can begin to reflect his character and likeness, which paves a discernable pathway to freedom. With Jesus as our perfect example, we were given the blueprint for being set free. Jesus said, for example, that as we embody His standards and lifestyle, His truth will set us free.

Jesus confirms and promises that He (alone) provides the solution to end all our suffering, oppression, and bondage. The question then arises: "Why do so many who've accepted Jesus still suffer with insufferable levels of bondage and oppression?" Surveys show that within the population of people who claim to have accepted Jesus, there is a persistent and significant increase in unbridled lust/sexual immorality, pride, envy, covetousness, and greed (among countless other maladies). When it comes to issues driven by the corrosive and demonic culture, there seems to be no definitive contrast or notable difference between the level of participation of Christians as compared to non-Christians/"unbelievers." Everyone (whether Christian or not) seems to be stricken by the bondage and oppression of the world system; most everyone is succumbing to "the matrix!"

The truth: Not everyone is in bondage, but since there are so few living a victorious life freed from bondage, it seems like a pervasive reality for everyone. Our foe (satan) uses lies and deceptions intertwined throughout culture to create a false narrative that bondage is pervasive and inescapable. Even though it consistently manifests aggressive forms of demonism, culture is still largely being embraced by those whom Jesus wants to set free. The crux of our suffering can be distilled down to the understanding that we cannot embody Jesus' freedom while also in the embrace of the trappings of world systems. This is impossible. We must accept Him and reject the other (the world/cultural forces) since they are polar opposites. The acceptance and embrace of the world system (matrix) signifies we are aligned and intertwined with it and in need of deliverance. Fundamentally, we must find ways to reject the world and cleave to Jesus in order to arise from our fallen state.

Humanity "hangs in the balance" and must decide which "freedom" it wants. The decision point boils down to whether it is more desirable to experience a veneer of freedom (unbridled variations of anger, lust and pride) while continuing in the abusive oppressions of the world system. Or, is the desire to be truly free and wholly unbound from the wiles of this world by being connected and dependent on God and His Kingdom? Irrespective of how this question is answered, the only option for being "freed" is an unwavering embrace of truth! It is the truth (alone) that sets people free.

It is clear humanity has fallen, but we can get up; we can arise! Our creator has extended a clarion call for freedom. It is now time to depart from the bondage that has come with the fall of humanity and arise in order to be freed!

Two

"The truth, the whole truth, and nothing but the truth..."

Truth is oftentimes inconvenient. Whenever I grapple with inconvenient truths, my thoughts invariably turn to the impactful scenes from the movie "A Few Good Men" (1992). In this compelling movie, Colonel Nathan R. Jessup (portrayed by Jack Nicholson) finds himself in a courtroom, confronting a crucial inquiry about the truth—the unadulterated truth. The moment unfolds with poignant drama as Jessup poses the question, "You want answers?" The questioning lawyer responds assertively, "I WANT THE TRUTH!" with emphasis. In a memorable and emphatic retort, Jessup (Nicholson) declares, "YOU CAN'T HANDLE THE TRUTH!" This iconic exchange vividly captures the film's intensity, leaving an indelible impression as a powerful representation of confronting uncomfortable realities.

In the broader context, the reality we all must confront is that truth is sometimes inconvenient and undesirable. While we may profess a desire for the unvarnished truth, recognizing it as the key to liberation, we must also acknowledge the possibility that we may not be fully prepared to handle the truth. Facing this truth about our own limitations becomes a crucial aspect of our journey towards being truly set free.

The most insightful source that exposes all evils (and also provides solutions) confronting mankind is the Bible. Most would agree the Bible is a reliable source to glean knowledge and a more comprehensive understanding of truth, so the Holy Bible is the primary source to rely on for identifying and unpacking the necessary tools for being set free.

Biblical theologians and clergy have attempted to reconcile the truth of the Word of God with the daily realities of human existence for millennia. The Bible is replete with overarching themes and promises that followers of Christ will experience "life and that more abundantly," "being set free," "rest for your souls," "joy," and limitless "power" (among countless other promises). However, many who proclaim to be Jesus' followers experience a reality nowhere near what is promised. Many live a life of lack and constant turmoil, struggle with resentment, endure violence and hatred, and are overwhelmed with various forms of bondage and oppression. Why? How do we reconcile the truth of God's Word with the realities of our daily life? We are confident and know the Word of God is truth, so where is the breakdown? What are we missing?

When reviewing the issues of life and various plights affecting humanity, most suffering can be distilled down to the feeling of being stuck in some form of bondage. Whether physically bound or just in the mind (via oppression, depression, etc.), we live in a realm replete with bondage. The fact is, the world system (our cultural matrix) is designed to overlay and encourage bondage and enslavement. Our desire to break free while insidious cultural forces press upon us is the war that rages. We are in a cultural war, and there is only one way to disrupt the pattern of bondage and enslavement: His name is Jesus!

Jesus is the disruptive force. In John 14:6, Jesus says, "I am the way, the truth, and the life…" Jesus confirms that He is the path to God and salvation. Jesus is the embodiment of the ultimate truth. Jesus' transcendent truth is the disruptive force that eviscerates lies, deceptions, and bondage constitutive to the world system. Since it is the truth that sets mankind free, Jesus is the exclusive pathway to freedom. He alone sets mankind free. With innate human desires to be truly "set free," and recognizing that we can only be freed through Jesus, perhaps clergy/ministers need to include in their "salvation message" a sincere focus on how to be set free from all bondage. Bondage is systemic to this realm, encapsulating the world system. It is inescapable without liberation via the only disruptive force who sets mankind free: Jesus!

TRUTH ABOUT TRIALS AND TRIBULATION

After reflecting on the many challenges in life, an argument can be made that everyone is suffering (or has suffered) from some form of difficulty and bondage. Jesus makes clear that the world (world systems) is designed to produce tribulation (great trouble, suffering, difficulty). Broadly speaking, tribulation connotes prolonged difficulty, distress, and bondage, and it is assured for all. Mankind was forewarned of persistent trials and tribulation. John 16:33 confirms Jesus' assertion that "... In the world you will have tribulation..." Tribulations are not conditional or mentioned as a possibility; they are guaranteed. Jesus confirms it as a persistent reality!

All mankind faces tribulation, which can take on many forms. Some view work/career as producing tribulation and bondage. Some say raising a family with all its challenges produces a form of tribulation. Some say "skin color" and ethnicity produce some kind of tribulation. Some say having significant responsibilities just to manage all the "ups and downs" of life produces chaos and tribulation. We see people everywhere feeling like they're enduring tribulation of some sort as it manifests in the form of bondage and oppression.

If just listening to media reports, we would be under the impression most Middle Eastern countries are under intense tribulation and oppression. We would believe most ethnicities around the world are being oppressed. We would also hold that most who live in America ("home of the brave and land of the free") are not at all free and, instead, are oppressed and in bondage while suffering under the veneer of some sort of "supremacy." Are all these forms of tribulation and oppression valid? Or, is "the matrix" (world system) designed to produce cultural trends that encourage and reward hyper-emotionalism and the need to be perceived as a "victim" of myriad tribulations and bondages to instigate these feelings? Only God knows each individual's heart and intentions, but there are some basic truths that we can lean on to help discern and overcome all tribulations, including any forms of oppression and bondage. In the second part of John 16:33 verse, Jesus explains we receive the ultimate solution in overcoming tribulation when we put all our trust in Him, because He overcomes the world. It says, "...But take heart; I have overcome the world."

God is good, and His Son (Yeshua/Jesus) came with a fundamental objective "to set the captive free," so suffering insufferable bouts with feelings of being oppressed and in bondage is not due to Him. Our God designed humanity for human flourishing! Presenting the Gospel connoting human flourishing in the face of immense human suffering presents a bit of a conundrum, however. We know God is good, and we know the sufficiency of the Cross and all His Son has done to set us free, but too often, Christians are stuck in worsening human conditions that rampage globally. When stuck in what seems like unbreakable binds of the cultural matrix, we are enslaved and unable to break through and arise. Humanity's base condition is to be powerlessly enslaved to the world system. While recognizing whips and chains that dominated ancient forms of slavery have been (mostly) abolished, we can't deny there has been an exponential growth of pervasive mindsets bemoaning overwhelming feelings of bondage and oppression. These feelings confirm a level of relative enslavement to the world system, and it is our plight. But God! God provides the ultimate disruptive force as the solution to dismantle the "cultural matrix" we find ourselves in.

While there are notable forms of modern-day slavery that persist globally (i.e. sex slavery, child labor, and various forms and degrees of forced labor), most of the cries for the need to be set free from "oppressors" (often distinguished as being race-based, "colonialists" or "supremacists") come from people living in what are objectively understood to be free societies. Prevailing narratives dominating cultural and societal discourse are continuously urging that bondage, enslavement, and oppression are everywhere and in everything. Is it an aberration, or is it "real?" Is it possible that cultural whims and narratives are endued with grotesque generalizations, exaggerations, and false narratives, and are not designed to lessen but rather create and enable bondage? If that's the case, it would make sense that there is an increase in those claiming to be experiencing increased levels of oppression because there's been an exponential increase in hyperbolic claims and propaganda driving cultural narratives. Our foe (satan) designed and infused lies and deceptions to be disseminated throughout the cultural stream to produce enslavement. We are coming to realize that humanity is experiencing a cycle of unending and insatiable oppression and bondage driven by false narratives. These insidious cultural forces subsisting on negative emotions of chaos and hatred confirm we are fighting an unseen enemy who attacks and undermines our souls. It confirms we are fighting a spiritual battle in the battlefield of the mind.

Our conundrum is not that God is not doing anything to cure our plight and set us free. Rather, the relative malaise we sense is about insidious forces pushing humanity to the extent of "overwhelm" so that we are blinded to what God is doing. Our foe purposefully creates and encourages such chaos and overload because he knows God (alone) provides the solution that allows us to be freed.

Entire countries, regions, states, and individuals are bound and must be set free because the world is boiling. We need a solution to finally end pervasive and debilitating moods that overlay bondage and oppression onto entire cultures and societies. Groaning under undue pressure created by false narratives has led to increased chaos, division, and oppression, so finally putting an end to bondage and enslavement is now paramount. The solution is here. The solution is truth, and it is truth alone that provides the key to being set free!

KEY TO FREEDOM

The fall of mankind (in the Garden of Eden) has inculcated unbridled lies and deceptions that hold humanity in bondage. The only antidote to lies and deceptions is truth, and since Jesus is the truth, He delivers new root systems and foundations to help discern and unravel the bondage of falsehoods and deceptions. This is the process God has provided for setting men free. Jesus is the truth, the whole truth and nothing but the truth!

We note that truth is not just an act, a volition, or principled intuition; it is much more. It holds vital keys to life! We will see that the truth (Jesus) is the transformative force that unlocks the possibility for humanity to live life to its fullest and in abundance! When we discover and hold truth as a critical component of life, truth can no longer be ignored or dismissed as something "fluid" or relative.

Exposing the truth for what it is — and what it is not — is

easier to comprehend and appreciate when we can appropriately discern its opposite. Identifying the direct opposite of
truth solidifies the fundamentals and characteristics of actual
truth. That said, what is the opposite of the truth? Simply put,
the opposite of truth are lies, fallacies, myths, and fables. These
constructs are fundamental to schemes designed to deceive
by constructing false narratives. If these lies, false narratives,
and myriad forms of deceptions are embraced, an ecosystem
of entanglement that is tied to lies is developed. These ties are
literal binds that shape reality (albeit a contorted, perverted
reality). Simply put, individuals become tethered to systems of
bondage through entanglement with lies and false narratives;
this is the matrix we live in.

Our matrix is representative of vast systems generating
bondage and oppression wholly constructed out of foundations
of lies and deceptions. Some examples are tropes carrying
false narratives about Jews and Israel, for example, creating the
bondage of antisemitic hate as wars rage in the Middle East.
False narratives about "White Supremacy" instill the bondage
of hate, shame, guilt, and distrust for whites/Caucasians. False
narratives about America and colonialism create bondage of
carrying anti-American sentiment and the desire to destroy her
foundations and traditions. These are just a few examples of
some of the oppressive mindsets that a large percentage of
humanity carries as bondage, but there are endless examples of
false narratives and tropes that are infused in our cultural matrix.
This ecosystem is constituted in lies. The good news is there is
an antidote. The one and only antidote is truth...Yeshua/Jesus!

Think about it. Undisputedly, the Bible declares, "Truth will set us free." Since truth holds the key to setting us free, its opposite (a lie) must deliver the opposite. By definition, lies hold the key to establishing and keeping us in bondage. Get this: truth is freedom. Lies and deceptions are bondage!

MATRIX: ECOSYSTEM OF WORLDLY TRAPPINGS

Our cultural matrix is fundamentally rooted and designed to enshrine an ecosystem of bondage. This ecosystem is established through a network of broad entanglements, and they take root in people's lives through the embrace of false narratives, lies, and deceptions. Today, when there is a dearth of truth resulting from media omissions, propaganda, deceptions, and neo-Marxist cultural trends designed to deceive, lies are gratuitously overlaid onto entire cultures and societies, and large swaths of humanity experience bouts of oppressive hopelessness. This oppression and hopelessness is not new; it has consistently occurred for millennia. When hope fades, discouragement and rage become overarching moods for entire cultures and societies. Then hateful chaos ensues. The vicious cycle undermining humanity must end. Humanity yearns to be freed!

From the beginning of mankind (but after the fall of man in the Garden of Eden), there has been immense suffering, chaos, hatred, and various forms of oppression that have permeated humanity. Keep in mind that human sufferings were unleashed in conjunction with the fall of man. "The fall" resulted from rebellion against God and pivoted humanity onto a downward trajectory. Since then, the ontological design of man (man's "way of being") has been significantly altered. Ultimately, humankind began to enshrine lies and deception as overarching themes under the rulership of "the father of lies" (satan). And, since the Bible describes satan as "the god of this world," his lies and deception are the pervasive "native language" that he uses to hold humanity captive; falsities have been unleashed to precipitate continuous systems of bondage and oppression. This not only demonstrates we are not free, it fully demonstrates we are enslaved. This cultural matrix of brutal enslavement must come to an end.

WANTING AND ENSLAVED

From our beginning, the fall of man unleashed a diabolical pivot away from what God designed and ordained for humanity. Now, we have become slaves to an evil cultural matrix. To be sure, Romans 6:16 declares, "Don't you know that when you offer yourselves to someone as obedient slaves, you are slaves of the one you obey..." When we capitulate to socio/cultural whims dominated by gratuitous lies and deceptions, we become slaves to it. Discouragement, bondage, oppression and suffering of any kind are symptomatic of a plague of fundamental spiritual issues that need to be dealt with. Ironically, mankind has mostly ignored schemes from our foe (satan), who holds us captive, and instead (under the auspices of his lies and false narratives), we blindly adopt his tactics and blame others for our suffering. When we come to recognize the truth of this matter, we will see that simplistic blaming and finger-pointing at others for perceived oppression and plight is often misguided and sophomoric, not principled. When we succumb to these tactics, we play into the hands of our foe as he further cements our enslavement and bondage to his demonic ends.

Fully embracing cultural narratives and sanctimoniously pointing fingers of condemnation and accusing others of our perceived bondage and oppression are actions motivated via lies and false narratives; again, these attitudes and actions are generated by "the father of lies." The good news is that the cycle of bondage ends when we are freed.

TRUTH VS DELUSIONS

Since the fundamental premise of this book is the pursuit of being "freed," the necessary method is to become adept at acknowledging and accepting objective "truth" (God's truth). Adolescent concepts and pretentious views that connote truth as subjective, relative, and conditional (only acknowledged and accepted to assuage the dictates of the individual) can no longer be tolerated or accepted. Marxist trends toward postmodernism assert subjectivity as the singular way to determine what is true and reliable for proper human actions. Conversely, principled truth in pursuit of being set free requires understanding that notions of "relative truth" are a grand delusion; since delusions are lies, that notion is a preeminent factor that prolongs and encourages bondage, not freedom.

We must begin to recognize that the truth that sets you free cannot tolerate schemes of purposeful self-delusion. Playing the "truth card" by stating platitudes and deflections about "living my truth" does not set us free. These sinful and fleshly delusions are designed to exponentially increase bondage (because delusions have to be defended, along with duplicitous hypocrisies). If it is not true, it is a lie; there is no "in-between." If we are sincere about breaking free of bondage, the truth that sets us free demands we identify and hold to principled and objective truth. Ultimately, we can eventually gain enough fortitude to wade through the muck of generations of deceptions to find the authentic self that God designed for us, and holding fast to that, we begin the process to be set free.

THE AUTHENTIC SELF

Acts 17:28 declares, "For in Him we live, and move and have our being..." (NIV). This Bible verse confirms that our true self is found in Christ alone; our authentic self can only (primarily and exclusively) be found in Him. He is our Maker. Therefore, He knows why He made us (our specific purpose), and He holds the key to our destiny. When we wholly embrace God's divine work in us, we can connect with truth. Through this relationship, we can discover the authentic self (the person and destiny God designed). Purposefully pursuing a relationship with God (and discerning His intentions for us, individually) is vital because, through this relationship, we are free from bondage. We can begin to produce healthy interactions through genuine and holistic connections grounded in truth. Our relationships improve because they are grounded in truth (without hidden agendas and deceptions). It's these connections that allow us to live with authenticity and purpose. Said differently, truth unleashes the infrastructure of truth that establishes and surrounds us; it insulates us from the world system/matrix. Truth alone encourages sincere relationships that ultimately destroy bondage and oppressive sufferings.

FREED INDEED

Jesus is the fulcrum truth that sets humanity free; this fact by itself is an undervalued (or misunderstood) truth. Humanity has endured tribulations and plagues for millennia, but few sources have produced the antidote to end manifest sufferings around the globe.

Mankind has been rutted and stuck in ecosystems of bondage (via cultural "matrix") due to the embrace of perpetual lies and deceptions, and this is what perpetuates people's inability to break cycles of oppression and victimization. Think about it; if we are living a "lie" (not consistently authentic and principled), by definition, we are not "free." Said differently, it is impossible to be free while living in the bondage and trappings of lies generated within our cultural matrix. Our foe uses "the matrix" to his advantage and keeps mankind in bondage by blinding us to reality: truth! With the blind acceptance of webs of lies and doctrines of demons, it has become commonplace to point fingers and blame others when feelings of victimization and oppression arise. In reality, the individual creates bondage by not cleaving to truth.

Before asserting that our ethnicity, upbringing, community where we live, economic circumstances, and perceived oppressive acts of others are the causes of our "lack," bondage and oppression, we should ask ourselves, "Am I living a lie?" "Could it be that I have not connected with my authentic self and divine purpose (only found in Christ) in order to be set free and live life in abundance?" While the pursuit of authentically living in truth is an important step to understanding and achieving freedom, many will still (no doubt) deceive themselves into believing lies that assert subjective or "personal truth" (i.e., "my truth"). Again, this only perpetuates self-deception and creates false narratives that restrict, inhibit, and imprison. The perfect recipe for languishing in bondage.

John 8:36 confirms, "If the Son sets you free, you are truly free"; freed indeed! We are coming to understand that the freedom to live life in its fullness can only begin when preoccupations with lies and deceptions end. Simply put, the life God promises can only be achieved with an unflinching and unwavering clutch on truth! Jesus (truth) must be wholly embraced, and all figments portending "my truth," "my lived experiences"/standpoint epistemology (focusing on one's "lived experiences" as the barometer of truth), must be rejected in order to overcome the perpetual bondage infused in this realm. Jesus is exclusive. He is not "a truth." He is "the truth!"

There is a binary of polar opposites at work between truth and lies. The only way to end our oppression, hate, animus, and chaos (based on the lies and deceptions of the world system/culture) is to reject the cultural matrix that's driving these narratives. There are no in-betweens. When people endure endless cycles of suffering, chaos, and oppression, it confirms there is a lack of truth. Since the entire globe is under a cloud of tribulation and bondage, we should ask, "What truths are being ignored or not accepted?" Has Jesus truly been accepted as "the way, the truth, and the life?" Has He been embraced as "the Son who sets us free indeed?" With humanity being assaulted by an unrelenting foe destined to destroy us, there is only one answer that allows us to finally triumph over the schemes of this world embedded with bondage and oppression. Jesus!

2 Cor. 2:14 declares, "…God always leads us to triumph in Christ…" If we believe God is all-powerful (omnipotent), and His Word is true, then we must realize He has already made a way for us to triumph. This means those who remain overwhelmed with feelings of oppression and bondage do so because they have not accepted and yielded to the truth, the whole truth, and nothing but the truth. They are making accommodations and equivocating at some level with lies and deceptions. What is most telling about our dire situation is the fact that many churches and entire denominations are seemingly more divided now than ever before over issues of "oppression," racism, and the need for reparations. These conversations indicate spiritual bondage, we must ask, what false narratives have they adopted that hold them spellbound?

THE CULTURAL MATRIX AND PULPITS
Many people seem compelled to comport to grotesque false narratives woven into the cultural tide of the world system. Thus, we see religious dominations and congregations that persist in bondage to bitterness, discord, and disunity. According to

recent Barna Reports, each new generation brings less reliance on and belief in God, and more reliance on cultural worldviews.[2] George Barna Research Report on Millennials 2021 reveals that we are living in the most Godless generation on record. Based on Barna's research, one/third of Millennials identify as members of the LBGTQ community, 54% admit the presence of mental illness and 33% don't know, care, or believe in God. Barna concludes that the absence of a Biblical Worldview is the primary cause of their condition. This is a prelude to the reality that it is not only Millennials being grossly affected by our ever-corrosive culture/world system, but it also indicates erosion of spiritual conditions within younger and older generations; they are not seeking Biblical truths! Due to the toxic cultural tide, there are many contemporary issues fueling false narratives that captivate and compel perpetual bondage (tethered to "the matrix").

It becomes apparent Christians are not having open and loving dialogs with other Christians seeking truth. Instead, we see people of faith lecturing each other from polarizing ideological (or political) frames, or just choosing to remain silent and complicit. Unfortunately, hyper-partisan polarization has taken over many church pulpits. In many cases there is complete silence from the pulpit as myriad cultural issues gain preeminence while purposefully targeting to undermine faith institutions. Addressing what is happening in culture seems off-limits for most pastors. If there is a sermon from the pulpit addressing culture, it's typically purposefully watered-down for fear of offending those with cultural sensibilities.

According to findings from the American Worldview Inventory 2022, just slightly more than a third of pastors/clergy (37%) have a Biblical worldview and the majority—62%—embrace a hybrid worldview known as syncretism. This all-new national survey of pastors also evaluates worldview based upon pastoral positions within the church. Among senior pastors, four of 10 (41%) have a Biblical worldview. Next highest was 28% among associate pastors. Fewer than half as many teaching pastors (13%) and children's and youth pastors (12%) have a Biblical worldview. Executive pastors recorded the lowest level of biblical worldview—only 4% have consistently Biblical beliefs and behaviors. Lowest of all is a category that should have been at the top the list: beliefs and behaviors related to the Bible, truth, and morality. This category shows only 39% of pastors possess a biblical worldview in this area. By far, less than half of pastors live consistent with Gods Word! This is the crux of why there is manifest tribulation and suffering within churches. Most often, pastors/clergy don't believe what they preach because they are caught up in the matrix. While a demonic brew of grotesque dysfunction dominates culture, it silences the church. Sermons encouraging to live a life of abundance and rest in Christ can't come from most pulpits because most pastors don't fundamentally believe such a life is attainable.

Since the culture is infused with gratuitous lies and deceptions, many clergy and religious institutions act more like "cultural and spiritual relativists." That means they view norms and values as relative/subjective and only understood within a cultural context, i.e., cultural acquiescence and appeasement rather than adhering to strict Biblical orthodoxy. Nefarious cultural factions and trends have infiltrated the church, encouraging and precipitating disconnection (instead of engagement) and angst toward others (instead of tolerance and respect). Unity has not resulted. Unfortunately, many church people have been promoted and catapulted into ministry based on personality and charisma, and view ministry as a platform to advance personal ambition (building their own kingdom/fiefdom and following) and make money. A man-centered cult of personality (undergirded by great "motivational speakers," not Biblical teachers who disciple) drives much of the dysfunction in Christendom. Impotence ensues. The church grows impotent and cannot address moral decay because it is so much intertwined and a part of it. Unless ministries and ministry personalities (clergy) submit under Lordship (to the extent it becomes the clear Christian standard), continued impotency and failures in ministry are assured.

Countless factions and divisions now proliferate within the church. A lack of harmonious flourishing within the church is a result of differing opinions and beliefs about who God is and what He is doing. Current trends (buttressed by false narratives) have precipitated the embrace of syncretism, faith "deconstruction," and the infusion of cultural Marxism. All feelings of futility and nihilism (Marxian fundamentals) are instruments of satan designed to undermine truth (Christ) and enshrine lies and deceptions. Most troubling is these antithetical discourses have exponentially increased bondage and oppression within the body of Christ instead of allowing the people to be freed through Jesus. Cultural degradations indicative of the world system, like domestic violence, serial adulterers, and homo-sexualism/lesbianism, represent just some of the major bond-ages that continue unabated in our churches. In short, even (and especially) within communities of faith, there is a lack of commitment to hold truth (Jesus) and reject sociocultural false narratives!

We fervently call for truth – the whole truth and nothing but the truth. However, it appears that living a life centered on Jesus introduces an inconvenient truth that many are reluc-tant to acknowledge. Recent research by George Barna sheds light on the prevailing chaos and dysfunction within church and faith communities. A disconcerting reality emerges: we have succumbed to illusions prevalent in the cultural matrix. While false narratives and delusions are not the truth we aspire to, the widespread suffering from bondage and oppression globally serves as undeniable evidence that we have embraced them.

The question arises: why this embrace? There exists a cer-tain allure in participating within the cultural milieu. It seems to bestow status and relevance, proving to be seductive. Much like the narrative in a movie, we find ourselves entangled in the cultural matrix, tethered to its influence. This underscores the critical need for true deliverance, breaking free from the allure of cultural seduction. The key lies in becoming tethered to our "cultural disruptor" and deliverer – Jesus!

Three

Freed "to be," or not to be?...
That is the question!

Confronting a pivotal moment in life brings to mind the essence of Shakespeare's Hamlet, particularly the renowned quote "To be or not to be." This phrase encapsulates the universal human struggle with life's challenges and the uncertainties that loom ahead. The phrase "to be or not to be" presents a fundamental dilemma of whether it is nobler to endure the myriad struggles of life or to opt for the unknown realm of death and nonexistence. This question encompasses themes of life, death, morality, and the human condition. Likewise, are we "freed to be," "or not to be," is a question each person must ask themselves about being truly set free. Real freedom is wholly attainable, but it comes at a "cost." In truth, freedom is not "free."

The truth is, freedom lives! We have the freedom to indulge in cultural trends like nihilism, humanism, secularism, and atheism and all the bondage that comes with them. We have the freedom to indulge in pornography, avarice, and hedonism of all kinds. These freedoms also bring insatiable appetites, driving needs, addictions – all traps. We have the freedom to hate people based on their perceived "privileges" or based on skin color, but while expressing these hates may satisfy a kind of lust, it also leads to the bondage of jealous and covetous hearts. Bondage has been purposefully infused into anything and everything that we would want because of the world system(s)/cultural matrix we are a part of. An excellent description of the world system appears in 1 John 2:16: "For everything in the world—the lust of the flesh, the lust of the eyes, and the pride of life—comes not from the Father but from the world." Accordingly, anything and everything that feeds our *lust* binds us to fleshly strongholds. Along with *pride* (the principal malady that severs us from God), lust and pride together represent mortal sins upon which all sins are rooted. Our foe (satan) has strategically designed lust and pride (self-aggrandizement is found in both) as tethers intertwined onto oppressive ecosystems with unlimited tentacles that lead to bondage. These are the principal strongholds that enslave mankind.

With the fall of man, the world has pivoted into a "slave state." Since the fall of mankind, everyone has been born into sin and has become a slave to it. It is inescapable. That means the "normal" preeminent state of mankind suffers under the entanglement of lies and deceptions that lead to unending bondage and oppression. Yes, God has given men free will, but free will doesn't amount to much if most are blinded to their existing bondage and are deluded to embrace it out of the exercise of their "free will."

MANKIND PERSONIFIES ENSLAVEMENT

God created all human beings and provided free will with a binary choice. This means there are only two sides ("good"/freedom and "evil"/oppressive bondage), and all created beings have the ability to choose. The angelic hosts have free will, and one-third rebelled against God exercising it. Humans have free will, live in rebellion, and (generally) are blinded to the binary choice; they experience inextricable bondage because of it.

Freedom is the operative component of free will, but due to the innate maladies of pride and lust permanently infused into this fallen realm, most are blinded and have misconstrued the true meaning and understanding of freedom. Many see freedom in terms of being unrestricted, uninhibited, and unrestrained. The reality is we are born into bondage, so these distinctions are misnomers. Constraints are ever-present in realms where evil strongholds and bondage persist. For example, if someone indulges to the extent they rely on excessive use of drugs and alcohol, wild partying, and addictive relationships, the desire to participate in these activities becomes the constraint and bondage that prevents freedom to choose otherwise. While many activities (encouraged by culture and world systems) may feel "freeing" and unrestrained, they are designed to become an entanglement in and of themselves that cannot relieve pain, loneliness, suffering and bondage. Instead, they are designed to exacerbate these feelings.

If someone enjoys gambling, carousing or similar activities of unrestrained avarice, the desire to participate in these activities becomes a constraint when at various times it is not possible to participate in them. Bondage and suffering become oppressive, and this is the outcome of an elaborate ecosystem designed to produce delusions, lies and endless deceptions. The fallen world system cannot provide true freedom (as defined as being free from bondages) because it is designed to inculcate bondage and oppression. True freedom is wholly impossible within the confines of the world system. The only antidote to bondage is to be freed by truth.

The truth about freedom as we define it is that it is not freedom in reality. We are slaves. We are either slaves unto sin or unto righteousness, but our enslavement is sure. In essence, the only freedom we have is the freedom to choose our master. The binary choice is to choose sin or righteousness, but the truth is we cannot escape being a slave to something. In Romans 7:14, Apostle Paul puts it this way: "...The trouble is with me, for I am all too human, a slave to sin." Paul confirms that with just the act of being born, we are delivered into a realm that inculcates sin; it's inescapable! If we're born into sin, we commit sin; this, too, is inescapable! John 8:34 confirms Jesus as saying, "Very truly I tell you, everyone who sins is a slave to sin." With being born into sin, we are (by default) slaves to sin.

The default human condition is being a slave to sin! 2 Peter 2:19 says, "They promise freedom, but they themselves are slaves of sin and corruption. For whatever overcomes a person, to that he is enslaved." This confirms that since we are born into sin and participate in the world systems, we are enslaved to it. Romans 6:16 (NLT) confirms, "Don't you realize that you become the slave of whatever you choose to obey? You can be a slave to sin, which leads to death, or you can choose to obey God, which leads to righteous living." Thank God to have been provided the freedom to choose; we are free to choose whether we want to live as a slave to bondage (money, sexual immorality, drugs, and avarice of all kinds) or whether we want to be set free as a slave to righteousness!

The message of truth and freedom is clear. We are born into a fallen world of sin. Sin develops as an ecosystem of bondage that seduces, promotes and masquerades itself as "freedom." But, since the soul is bound, the veneer of freedom actually delivers slavery. Jesus came to set us free, and since mankind has the ability to choose between the polar opposites of truth vs. lies, good vs. evil, and oppression vs. freedom, we have the ability to choose to be set free from the bondage of sin by accepting Jesus as our Lord and Savior. *Anyone can be set free through Jesus.* So, the truth is that freedom as we envision and desire it can only be achieved through a relationship with Christ.

Galatians 5:1 says, "It is for freedom that Christ has set us free. Stand firm, then, and do not be encumbered once more by a yoke of slavery." The world system is constantly pushing its agenda to enslave. And, by definition, systems wholly built on lies do not and cannot provide freedom of any sort. *Freedom requires truth.* Again, this is the reason that it is impossible for the world system we are born into to produce what can be defined as freedom.

The illusion of freedom is produced and relied upon because the "god of this (fallen) world" specifically relies on lies and deceptions to control hearts and minds. Through an intricately seductive and compelling weave of lust and pride (the base of all sins), culture is intertwined into a sophisticated ecosystem of sin. This is then seductively promoted as a benefit of progress/progressivism and enlightenment, which is used to enshrine bondage and oppression via endless webs of lies and deceptions. We should begin to realize that with the complex structures purposely designed to create bondage, we inevitably become trapped into cascading levels of enslavement.

Being confronted with the severity and truth of our plight is humbling and sobering. The reality that without God there is no way out of brutal and unrelenting oppressive enslavement via the matrix, is a harsh reality. Leslie Fielder, an American literary and cultural critic and scholar, opines that there is a desolating weariness with trying to be men (mankind). He states, "God has been abolished by the media pundits and other promoters of our new demythologized divinity. We continue to insist that change is progress, self-indulgence is freedom and novelty is originality. In the circumstances, it's difficult to avoid the conclusion that Western man has decided to abolish himself, creating his own boredom out of his affluence, his own vulnerability out of his strength, his own impotence out of his own erotomania, himself blowing the trumpet that brings the walls of his own city tumbling down. Having convinced himself that he is too numerous, he labors with pill and scalpel and syringe to make himself fewer, thereby delivering himself the sooner into the hands of his enemies. And last, having educated himself into imbecility and polluted and drugged himself into a stupefaction, he keels over, a weary, battled old brontosaurus, and becomes instinct."[3] Mr. Fielder sadly observes that freedom as vainly pursued in the secular world loses its luster, and many die bereft of true meaning or purpose.

CHOOSING WITHOUT LOSING

The true purpose of mankind is to ultimately come to know and embrace "The Truth": Yeshua/Jesus. We must choose one of two viable routes. One utilizes lies and deceptions designed to unleash dogged bondage and oppression under the guise of freedom. And the other is literally designed to set captives free through the embodiment of unvarnished *truth*. The truth finally puts an end to oppression and bondage brought on by world systems. The good news is God, by His grace, provides us with choice. We can choose our preferred course in life and our destiny!

God loved us all so much that He gave us His Son (His birth, death and resurrection paid the price to set us free) to break all bindings and oppressions of this world in order to deliver our freedom to choose. Sincerely asking Him to replace our slavery to sin with slavery (actually, a joyful submission) to His righteousness is the critical step. In accordance with His plan, God made and specifically designed us (with destiny and purpose) to take the step of freedom in Jesus. While searching for answers to a burdensome life, many don't consider going to their maker (God) to get answers and be set free. Too often lies and deception that open the door to bondage and oppression become "second nature' and natural, so many reject taking the vital step to end their misery. God, our maker, knows why He made and designed us, so it's in Him we will find answers to overcome world systems.

"THE DESIGNER AND MAKER"
PROVIDES INSTRUCTIONS

At some point, we have all tried to put appliances or gadgets together without reading or understanding the instructions from the maker. It always turns into a mess. In the end, we end up with extra screws and clamps, some piece will be in backwards, and the item won't function as designed. This is typical when we attempt to assemble things without relying on the maker for instructions. When we consider a universal truth that *the more complex the entity, the more purpose and design is in it*, we should begin to understand that humans (the most complicated of all creatures) need specific instructions/directions from our maker in order to function properly. Logically, this is an inescapable truth.

A fish out of water dies, a tree without soil dies, and likewise, a man without ongoing connection (relationship) with his maker (God) dies. God is our natural environment and provides all that we need to flourish. Only through Him can we live. Our plight of trying to deal with bondage and oppression of this world without instructions from our maker is symptomatic of mankind's hubris and arrogance. God alone knows how He put us together and our exact purpose, so He knows how we must function to overcome this world. Since there are only two things that last forever, the Word of God and the souls of men, and God is in control of them, we have a desperate need to go to our creator and ask what He has in mind for us (individually).

Jeremiah 1:5 declares, "Before I formed you in the womb I knew you, before you were born I set you apart; I appointed you as a prophet to the nations." This passage confirms how God forms the most intricate details for each of us in the womb, He destines our purpose and provides life's pathways for us, and finally, He provides our eternal destiny in Him. We are formed, by, through, and to Him! God is our creator and holds our master plan, so He alone can deliver us and set us on the right path. Our post-biological and eternal destiny is found only in Him. This understanding clarifies why our attempts to "figure out," and chart life paths on our own terms are hubris and arrogance, not progress. Progress, in this regard, is an all-consuming lie! This is what produces the culmination (the nucleus) of cycles of insatiable dissatisfaction. Without God, we fight a losing cosmic battle, which becomes winnable only when we redouble the commitment to strictly rely on God. Again, Acts 17:28 confirms, "For in Him we live and move and have our being." Without God, there are no answers to our bondage (in the form of oppression, depression, addictions, and any of the sufferings that overwhelm us). But, in Him, the chains of bondages of the world systems are broken, and we discover our entire pathway and destiny. In Him, our destiny is provided without the gratuitous lies and deceptions that bombard us found in the world system. In Him, we become slaves (of righteousness) and are truly set free once and for all.

In essence, we possess the freedom to embrace the fullness of what God created us to be. However, this liberation necessitates breaking free from the various oppressions and bondage that result from being ensnared by culture and its associated world systems. A crucial choice stands before us – whether to turn to the Master who crafted and ordained our destiny, or persist in being tethered to the lies and deceptions that foster oppressive bondage from the "god of this world." One choice unleashes the freedom to fully embody God's creation, while the other ensures a life perpetually mired in despair.

Opting for abundant life and freedom requires a deliberate exchange of masters. The foundational freedom bestowed upon everyone is the freedom to choose – either to persist in bowing to the master of lies and deceit or to begin bowing to the Master of truth who liberates us. The choice is profound and holds the key to our destiny. Choose wisely…

Four

Cultural Exodus: Leaving Matrix of Enslavement for Joyful Enjoinment with Christ

There is an urgent call for an exodus from the clutches of our culture and its corrosive constraints imposed upon humanity. We must break free from the enslavement to the cultural matrix (exodus) to embrace the joyful existence promised in Christ. Christ and our demonic culture cannot coexist.

A notable historical exodus is evident in the story of Moses leading his people out of Hebrew slavery into the promised land. A more recent example is the Great Migration of the early 20th century, a pivotal chapter in American history that reshaped millions of lives and transformed the demographic landscape of the nation. This migration was a response to harsh conditions and systemic racism prevailing in the Southern states. Jim Crow laws, racial segregation, and limited economic opportunities compelled African Americans to seek better prospects elsewhere. The promise of employment, improved living conditions, and the prospect of escaping the oppressive racial climate became the catalyst for this mass movement. Through resilience, determination, and the pursuit of a better life, the Great Migration stands as a testament to the enduring spirit of those who sought to break free from shackles injustices of the past, to abandonly pursue the promise of righteousness and justice in the future.

In contemporary times, akin to the era of the Great Migration, a palpable yearning exists among individuals to liberate themselves from the clutches of an enslaving and corrosive culture. This requires an exodus from the cultural matrix. This cultural exodus mirrors the journey of yesteryears, propelling individuals toward the joyful embrace of freedom found in Christ. This parallel odyssey underscores the timeless quest for freedom, fueled by the innate human desire to transcend present tribulations and embrace the liberating spirit found in Christ our Master.

Eternal truth confirms that everyone must make a definitive choice about who will be their master. This choice bears consequences of eternal cosmic proportions. This choice is individual (everyone must choose for themselves) and inescapable. In essence, we can choose to be hounded, tethered and bound as a slave to the world that we are born into. Or, we can choose to trust God to be delivered as an unrestricted, freed, and flourishing slave unto righteousness in His Kingdom. With the righteous Master/Jesus/Yeshua (literally defined as "to deliver, save or rescue), as our Lord, we will be lovingly ushered into overcoming the world as we yield ourselves with the expressed desire to pattern our lives after His.

To escape this world's bondage (cultural matrix) requires pivoting toward being set free in Christ Jesus should not be a difficult decision. It should be liberating to consider that all of the bondages (including addictions) and oppressions (including thoughts of suicide, covetousness, and hate for others) can be dealt with by simply making a choice for a different master. It is perplexing: Why haven't the communities of Faith unflinchingly taught the need for each purpose to take a stand, to make the simple binary choice that ensures the release and rejection of oppressive bondage? This is the Gospel, the good news and a simple truth, yet it seems it's not really understood. Why not? Perhaps it's because the world is under a spell and, therefore, has been gratuitously blinded to this reality.

An insidious spell (as in witchcraft) has been loosed and widely cast over the entire globe; it has held mankind captive for millennia. Since the rebellion with the fall in the Garden of Eden, the world has rebelled against God's natural order. Since that time, we have been under a form of significant witchcraft. Lies, deceptions, and witchcraft have blinded and sullied mankind's hearts and minds. The Bible says it like this in 1 Samuel 15:23: "For rebellion is as the sin of witchcraft, and stubbornness is as iniquity and idolatry." This verse confirms that rebellion is opposition to the will of God, and this act is akin to divination. The world has experienced a divining spirit since the fall of man. This spirit sets up bondage/strongholds that compel the binding of the soul to world systems, indeed a rejection of God and His divine order. Most people experience blind subserviency to a purposely destructive, detestable fallen world system where there is no hope. Its fundamental objective is to cast bondage and oppression on mankind. Once internalized as "reality," it is idolized. We arrive at a point in human history when culture is idolized and embraced as the creative source of ambition, freedom, and truth. This is the ultimate deception, and for those who embrace deceptions, deception is their plight. Regrettably, everyone faces this inescapable plight without our Savior (Yeshua).

Christ the Savior provides the key to freedom. Will we be free in Christ, the one who made and purposes us? Or will we settle for languishing in the bondage of worldly "freedom" that subsists on hate, rage, discord, and all manner of manifest evils? Even if the world gives the veneer of practicing freedoms with unfettered and reckless abandon, is yielding to demonism or a demonic system (like humanism, secularism, Marxism) actually indicative of being free? Or is it confirmation of bondage to demonism? An honest answer to this question, with sincere introspection, will help confirm that yielding to demonism in any form is bondage. Therefore, the world system is infused with unlimited instruments of bondage. The only way to break free of this bondage is to become a servant and slave, yoked to Jesus!

No matter how "simple" the transition away from being enslaved by the world, to the proposition of now willingly yielding as a slave to righteousness in Christ, most people seem still to consider this process a "heavy-lift." World systems have dominated our humanity and focus by encouraging self-aggrandizement through persistent humanist, secularist thinking. There are countless lies and deceptions continually reinforcing the human psyche with messages paying homage to "self." That's the rub.

When the "self" (under the ruse of personal autonomy) is undergirded and motivated by pride and lust (mortal sins), it is euphemistically enshrined on its own "throne"; it then becomes quite unsettling to relinquish control and bow in subjection to another. Since satan disguises the fact that when we are born we are delivered into submission to his enslavement, we don't readily want to think about relinquishing control of our "way of being" (e.g., pride, lust, anger, fear, etc.).

The truth is, irrespective of riches and glory (personal or political power), mankind has never been in control. Conversely, *mankind has been wholly controlled and enslaved mostly by oppressive thoughts about being in control.* This is a conundrum that can never be reconciled until we come to the end of ourselves. When we recognize the enslavement to world systems causes bondage and oppressions, and the escape is only possible when we lay down our life in obedience to the creator and Master, then we can be set free. That's a vital step toward freedom. So, now: "How exactly do we do that?"

As noted, mankind is in the midst of an eternal cosmic battle that predates us. In this realm, the battle is being waged through mankind, but it is very much a spiritual battle. In the spirit, some are slaves to sin resulting in bondage, oppression and death, while others are slaves of God, resulting in freedom and eternal life. In reality, everyone is a slave and tethered to spiritual powers greater than they are. Blind pride in full embrace of superficial significance doesn't win in this battle. Likewise, cultural trends that bind mankind to humanism, secularism and atheism (e.g., Marxism) are defiant strongholds and must be broken. This cosmic spiritual battle is won in brokenness, however, not defiance.

What is the value of gaining the entire world, indulging in worldly passions, and yielding to emotions of pride and lust, if it leads to the loss of your soul for eternity? There is no true gain in this! The sole solution to the spiritual battle rooted in the human plight is to attain freedom by being yoked to our Master. This represents the only pathway that allows a lasting exodus from cultural entanglements.

Embarking on a cultural exodus necessitates embodying the truth that liberates us, transforming us into servants and slaves of righteousness. In this, we commit to surrendering under the yoke of Jesus, thereby lightening the burden of the commitment to serve others. Though the process may sound circular and counterintuitive, committing to being yoked to Master Jesus to serve under His Lordship is the very essence of being set free to serve others. It is indeed a unique pathway.

A precise understanding of the terms "servant" and "slave" (in relation to Yeshua) will shed light on the process used to ultimately break free (exodus) from the insidious cultural matrix.

Five

The Master: He beckons, He invites, He promises and... He never fails!

Liberating oneself from the insidious demands of our corrosive culture is achieved solely through Jesus. Few individuals exemplify mastery in this area, and when I reflect, only two come to mind as true exemplars in this regard- my friends Larry Wiens and Dean Nelson.

This book is a tribute to the memory and lasting impact of Larry D. Wiens and Bishop Dean Nelson. These individuals epitomized Christ-centered marketplace leadership, ministry leadership, discipleship, and exhibited Godly and biblical character in every domain. They served as exemplary models, embodying the spirit of Apostle Paul's encouragement to "follow me as I follow Christ." Their irreplaceable loss is keenly felt by the world.

Reflecting on their lives, it is evident that they wholeheartedly embraced humility, willingly becoming servants and slaves under the Lordship of Christ. Notably, they radiated contagious joy, seeking only to bring glory to God in every endeavor. Even as their physical bodies faced challenges and ultimate frailty in their last days on earth, they remained unwaveringly loving and joyous. Their ability to express "no regrets" and exude abundant love, joy, and peace during the transitions of life stemmed from their deep connection to the Master. Having long ago detached from the world system, they were firmly yoked to the Master, Yeshua. It was the promises of the Master that empowered them to transcend the limitations of this transient life. In celebrating their legacy, I find inspiration in their unwavering commitment to a higher purpose and the profound peace that comes from being anchored in the promises of the Master. Larry and Deans lives illuminated how to escape the cultural matrix by embodying the subtle yet vital distinction between living as a servant of the Lord and simultaneously embracing the role of a slave to the Master. It was not an either-or scenario but a simultaneous and harmonious intertwining of both roles.

The Biblical definition of a servant, as compared to a slave, confirms they are similar in concept but, in practice, nuanced. A servant can be defined as a paid laborer; someone who expects compensation or benefit. A slave can be defined as one who is compelled to commit to a master (lord) without demand or expectation of recompense. In a way, we can say accepting Jesus with the heart of servant may carry expectations to gain eternal life and salvation (via Jesus as Savior). Committing as a slave to Jesus, however, is one who humbly commits to the Lordship of Christ out of the volition of the soul due to a compelling love and desire for Him alone. Likewise, accepting

Jesus because He is good, He is perfect, and He is worthy, and having no expectation for anything else is indicative of Lordship. Simply: "If He does nothing else for me, He is still good and worthy of all my praise."

Some think Jesus is merely sufficient for salvation (exclusively) but is not really approachable and applicable to help with every aspect and nuance of "life." This is a grand deception; Jesus commands we also accept His Lordship. Sincere followers of Christ committed to walking in fullness of truth, can only develop into the character and likeness of Yeshua by yoking to Him and becoming both His servant and slave.

Human sensibilities can get in the way of making the transition to becoming a slave to Jesus. Typically, our mind shifts to images of slavery as incorporating abusive, corrosive, and purposely oppressive acts intended to malign and undermine one's humanity. In our own feeble minds, envisioning a master who is *not* vengeful, abusive, and compulsive is really a stretch, but that is our Master (Yeshua). He's loving and continues to give the choice whether to stay with Him as a loving Master or revert back to being mastered by the abusive tenets of the world system. This adds complexity because when we accept Jesus, we come to know Him as a loving Friend, then we have to transition that understanding into the realm of a "Master-slave" relationship. The biggest distinction is that we are already being enslaved by an abusive and oppressive world system (and the "god of this world") by default. When we become slaves to Jesus, we are asking Him to be the Master of our lives because we realize we need Him (to be set free) and can do nothing (useful, productive, and God-honoring) without Him. Likewise, since He made us, we recognize a vital need for His Lordship!

We are born in and enslaved by endless entanglements to the world system. We are then coerced by culture, traditions, etc., to remain tethered to the abusive agitations leading to oppression and bondage in the world system. Conversely, Jesus invites us into a life of abundance and freedom (of the soul – mind, will and emotion) that cannot be produced outside of Him. The desire for "rest" and true freedom compels us into a Master/slave relationship with the Lord. In the book of Matthew 11:28-29, Jesus says it this way, "Come unto me, all ye that labor and are heavily laden, and I will give you rest. Take my *yoke* upon you, and learn of me; for I am meek and lowly in heart: and ye shall find *rest* unto your souls." Jesus beckons and invites us to come to Him. He confirms knowing the toil and intensely abusive agitation that makes our hearts groan with heaviness created by the world system. But, He promises He is not a taskmaster, is sensitive to our need for rest, and is humble enough to share in working with us (via the yoke).

As our Creator and Master, Jesus/Yeshua makes a promise only He can keep; He promises "rest" (peace) for our weary souls. This is comforting and compelling! Promises made directly from the One who loves us, created us and will keep us, is why we intentionally choose to shift away from being enslaved to a demonic system (designed by our foe who hates us and does all he can to steal, kill and destroy), to becoming a willing and grateful slave to Jesus!

Of the many fundamental tenets of the Bible, *the Lordship*

of Jesus has received little attention but in truth it is paramount and must become a focus. Cultural and religious traditions have focused on helping many understand what it means to be "saved" and inherit salvation by becoming a servant to Jesus. Yet they have all but ignored Lordship. For millennia, there have been countless sermons encouraging the need to accept Jesus Christ in order to receive an "eternal insurance policy" or to prevent eternity in "hell"; many denominations and clergy repetitively sermonize based on this aspect, so the view of Jesus is somewhat skewed. Of course, the salvation message is essential, but an overarching focus on salvation by becoming a servant of Christ, without encouraging the blessing of grace and freedom that comes from becoming a slave yoked under His rulership and authority (His Lordship), can prevent breaking the world systems' bondage. Lies and deceptions proliferate and are perpetuated under bondage and oppression of the world system unless there is full and humble embrace of Jesus' Lordship. Since Jesus is the Truth, the truth is that He is *both* our Savior and Lord, not one or the other. When He is acknowledged as Savior and Lord, we can receive the fullness of His promises for rest and freedom by overcoming the world system. If He is not Lord, we languish and suffer.

With the truth about being yoked to Jesus and being enslaved unto the Lordship of Christ has (largely) not been emphasized, a clash between Jesus' church and the demonic culture is now raging. Many churches and Faith institutions (generally) have begun to accommodate and show deference to culture along with its manifest lies and deceptions.

Since lies and deceptions are deeply woven into culture and cultural trends, the inculcation of cultures' oppressive bondage now deeply impacts the overall mood and tenor of the church body. The Church's authority and mission lose persuasiveness and power. More than ever, we're seeing increased division, distrust, and hateful rhetoric tearing Faith institutions asunder.

The embrace of lies and deceptions infused within cultural discourse has culminated into significant trends towards inter-denominational strife, syncretism (purposeful syncretizing and watering down of the Gospel message in deference to emerging cultural trends), race/ethnic intolerance, increased guilt and condemnation, "faith deconstruction," and embrace of neo-Marxist theologies (among myriad other issues). Much of the faith community has been infiltrated and undermined by cultural schemes enshrining the world's bondage and oppression systems. Instead of the church being recognized as a healthy institution with solutions to help people overcome tribulations of the world, it has become part of the world and therefore viewed as largely irrelevant. But all is not lost.

The good news is that while cultural secularism/demonism rampages even within the church, we are assured there is a way out. Jesus confirms, "I am *the way*, the *truth* and the *life*." We must become truth-bearers! The only *way (Jesus)* to assuredly overcome the many issues facing people of Faith is to embrace *the truth (Jesus)*, tethered to His (Jesus) *life*. This requires Jesus to become Savior and Lord.

THE BEGINNING OF THE END IS...US!

Bowing to the lordship of Jesus is easier said than done. It's a process, and the process can be difficult because it *begins* when we come to the *end* of ourselves. Perhaps that is why lordship is nowadays deemphasized. It is unnatural to desire to "end" the investment of personal identity (including our personal accolades and other testaments of vain glory) in deference to Christ. Most have spent countless decades scraping and striving to build identity, and now it is supposed to come to an end in Christ? What does that mean? What do we control if we submit our life (entirely) under the authority of Christ? How can He remake us? Will we still have money and resources? Will we still have personal accolades, influence and the glory of men?

Becoming yoked to Jesus and a slave to His will opens a world of unknown that seems unbridled and uncontrolled. The purposeful act of giving up control of our lives seems harrowing. In truth, however, it is not! It is the pathway to freedom.

It took me over a decade to come to the end of myself and just "trust God." It was challenging and exhilarating. And, it's still in process. My final surrender came when I realized I have absolutely no control over my money. No control over my future/destiny/legacy. No control over my family. Essentially, it boiled down to this: I have control of nothing and am nothing (without Him); God is everything! I felt God asking, "What can you control now? Are you in control of your next breath? Can you control your heartbeat or blood flow?" "You are here by My grace. I (God) can control everything, so trust Me!" This

49

dialog changed my life because it allowed me to understand my lack of power and exposed my delusion of believing in "my control." The truth is, I control nothing. It doesn't matter what I have worked so hard for, because if my next breath stops, it's all instantly meaningless. My pride, lust, and ambition were neatly wrapped in vain glory; it was vain because it was striving and pushing without God's plan and consideration of His pathway for me. A great example of a person documenting the process of coming to the end of himself (and yielding to God) is King Solomon. The story of King Solomon's life and his words of wisdom strongly resonate with me. Solomon said it best, when he proclaimed "vanity of vanities! All is vanity" (Ecclesiastes 1:2).

POWER OF GOD AND WISDOM OF SOLOMON COMPELS

God confirmed Solomon was the richest and wisest man to have ever lived. While having anything and everything at his disposal, Solomon lamented it's all a farce. He confirmed that human endeavors and achievements, apart from God, are ultimately empty (transitory). Solomon speaks to us that wealth, wisdom, pleasure, and other worldly pursuits are empty and indicative of worldly distractions. His call is for all mankind to recognize the only way to achieve fulfillment is to hang on tightly to God. Since He is your maker, He provides fulfillment and purpose for those who align with His divine wisdom and purpose. Solomon laments that all worldly pursuits are vanity and meaningless without God. The book of Ecclesiastes illuminates Solomon's insights on *ten worldly vanities*. Every notable domain of human activity is illuminated in his exposition of ten things that are utterly "meaningless."

Solomon says, without God, human *wisdom* is meaningless (2:14–16); *labor* is meaningless (2:18–23); amassing *things* is meaningless (2:26); *life* itself is meaningless (3:18–22); *competition* is foolish and meaningless (4:4); *selfish ambitions* is meaningless (4:7–8); *power and authority* are meaningless (4:16); *greed* is destructive and meaningless (5:10); *wealth and accolades* are empty and meaningless (6:1–2); and perfunctory *religion/religious activities (devoid of God's supreme influence and control)* is meaningless (8:10–14). It is understood that when Solomon characterizes "everything" as meaningless, he was not saying everything as having zero value. He had immense treasures of real value. He was affirming that everything, without (and outside of) God, has zero value; it's amounts to nothing and is meaningless!

Solomon, whom God proclaimed as the wisest man to have ever lived, was giving mankind a lesson confirming that apart from God's will (wholly overlaid and operating in every domain), all personal exploits, ambitions, accomplishments and tributes are void and utterly meaningless.

Reflect on the Most High God, His Son, and the richest and wisest man who has ever lived, all declaring that the only life worth living (a life having limitless eternal value) is the life submitted as a slave yoked to the Master. A commitment to serve the Lord as a servant (to gain the recompense of Heaven) is just a beginning step. The promised life of abundance (abundant joy, peace and well-being) and rest experienced within the Kingdom requires taking another step of submitting to the Lordship of Jesus and embracing His yoke as a slave. A surprising element we learn when coming under the Lordship of Christ is the realization that what we believe are manifest "freedoms" toward unfettered and unrestrained self-indulgence and gratification are literally chains of oppressions and servitude leading to nothingness; this is, of course, the antithesis of freedom. In its simplest and most basic terms, it's bondage.

This life, tethered to the world system, offers bondage under the auspices of "freedom," but true everlasting, eternal freedom comes *only* through being yoked with Christ! Solomon confirms you cannot be "free" (or experience freedom) while trapped within the bounds and limitations of human experience. Freedom comes from the soul (mind, will, and emotions), and God alone (our maker and King) holds the key to that level of freedom.

There are many examples of people compelled to accept Christ based on the promises of Heaven weighed against the threat of eternal separation in hell. While many still reject Christ, most see having their sins forgiven and the promise of eternal life (salvation) as a good reason to accept Christ. When salvation is the fundamental rationale for accepting Christ, without the necessity of dying to self and submitting our all to Christ (wholly controlled under His Lordship and authority), many experience what can be described as a superficial commitment. When the Lordship of Christ (a level of spiritual formation usually experienced through the process of discipleship) is ignored and not preeminent, the commitment to serve Him can become more superficial instead of supernatural. Supernatural anointing is what breaks enslavement to the world system, so promises of "rest," "abundance," and "peace" can be realized. Many have experienced becoming servant *to the institution of Christendom* (comporting to Faith traditions), rather than coming to the end of oneself in order to be yoked (as slave) to Jesus. This is a travesty leading to dire consequences.

Consider: Is it the Lordship of Christ that compels Christians to get divorced at virtually the same rate as secular unbelievers? God forbid! Is it the Lordship of Christ that increases the proliferation of "another gospel" like Liberation Theology/Black Liberation theology to be preached in pulpits? God forbid! Is it the Lordship of Christ that generates equivalent rates of sexual immorality/lust, abortions and greed as non-Christians? God forbid! Is it the Lordship of Christ that compels race/ethnic hatred and divisions, distrust and animus and neo-Marxist demands (from Clergy/Faith leaders) asserting unless reparations are paid, there can be no "unity?" God forbid! No indeed: Under the Lordship of Christ it is inconceivable any of the forementioned travesties would proliferate. These examples provide undeniably confirm many people of faith (and the church generally) are not compelled by the Lordship of Christ. The truth is, in almost every conceivable area, the Church mirrors the culture and underlying tenets of the world system. Sad. How does this happen? Well, this is to be expected when there has been misapplication and lack of understanding surrounding Jesus' command for Lordship!

Christian versus non-Christian statistics indicate that people of Faith (generally) embrace cultural trends of the world system (inclusive of lies and deceptions therein) at the same rate as secularists — instead of holding fast to the Biblical truth of the Gospel. More than anything, the troubling statistics confirm no distinction in the level of immorality between people professing to be followers of Christ, as compared to otherwise. Why? Perhaps the fantasy of dalliances infused into the world system are too compelling and the grip of cultural secularism/demonism too strong. But either way, the church wilts under unrelenting bondage. In his book *The End of Christendom*, Malcolm Muggeridge writes, "Built into a life is a strong vein of irony for which we should only be grateful to our creator. It helps us to find our way through the fantasy that encompasses us to the reality of our existence. God has mercifully made the fantasies – the pursuit of power, of sensual satisfaction, of money, of learning, of celebrity, of happiness – so preposterously unrewarding that we are forced to turn to Him for help and for mercy. We seek wealth, and we find accumulated worthless pieces of paper. We seek security and find we've acquired the means to blow ourselves and our little earth to smithereens. We seek carnal indulgence only to find ourselves involved in the prevailing erotomania. Looking for freedom, we infallibly fall into the servitude of self-gratification, or collectively, of a Gulag Archipelago (metaphorically, forced labor in an unending imprisonment)."[4] Malcolm Muggeridge's exposition is profoundly spot on! The way out of unending imprisonment to the bondage of the world system is to become yoked with Christ.

GETTING "YOKED"

A slang term used to signify having well-defined muscles (very muscular) and being in great shape, is "yolked." Metaphorically, the slang term yolked can be used to analogously signify becoming Spiritually well-defined and put in great Spiritual shape. While clever similitudes and metaphors can be devised, and realizing "yolked" and yoked sound similar, being yoked (in biblical terms) is quite different. Becoming yoked, biblically, provides incomparable transcendent qualities. In Matthew 11:29-30, Jesus encourages, "Take my yoke upon you and learn from me, for I am gentle and humble in heart, and you will find rest for your souls. For my yoke is easy and my burden is light." Jesus wants to be yoked with us. Our Maker wants relationship and fellowship.

An actual yoke used in agriculture is a mechanism used to join two animals, usually oxen, together to work as a team. When the Bible mentions being "yoked with Jesus," it implies a close connection as in "you see what He sees, you go where He leads, and you learn as He teaches." It powerfully indicates an intimate spiritual connection and relationship with Him. A person who is yoked with Jesus aligns with His teachings and guidance, and since Jesus does the directing, the person yoked receives spiritual rest and a sense of ease. The primary motivation is to yield oneself as a vessel to be led and guided, and to please Him (aligning with His Words). It means we rely on Jesus' Lordship to learn from Him how to take on and overcome issues while taking care of the mundane responsibilities of life. Lordship begins when the homage to self/our flesh "ends" (inclusive of trappings to lies and deceptions of the world systems). In the pursuit and pathway of Lordship, being "crucified with Christ" takes on real and tangible meaning.

THE CRUX OF ABUNDANT LIFE IS CRUCIFIXION

We've heard many sermons about "crucifying the flesh," but practically speaking, what does this mean? "Crucifying the flesh" and "living a crucified life" means that we arrive to a point when we are no longer driven by our five senses and fickle emotions constantly being triggered and agitated by our flesh; it means, we submit ourselves to the process of being "crucified with Christ," and to the extent Christ establishes and lives His life through us. Apostle Paul says it this way, "I have been crucified with Christ; it is no longer I who live, but Christ lives in me; and the *life* which I now live in the flesh I live by faith in the Son of God, who loved me and gave Himself for me." (Galatians 2:20 NKJV). In this passage, Paul describes the crux of what it means to live an abundant crucified life in Christ. This life involves a process. The process we must go through closely parallels the process of Jesus' crucifixion.

The commitment to follow Jesus is a commitment to untether from the world systems and follow His pattern in order to become a reflection of His character and likeness. As a final act and in His last breath, Jesus called out with a loud voice, "'Father, into your hands I commit my spirit.' When he had said this, he breathed his last." (Luke 23:44-46). Jesus' last words confirm complete faith and submission to Father (God). When we come to the end of ourselves and end our reliance on culture/matrix, we confirm this model of trust and reliance on God; understanding we are nothing with Him, we entrust and submit our lives to His divine care and sovereignty. It is supposed to be that Jesus lives through mankind (with man as a willing vessel/slave for producing His glory in the earth). Again, Apostle Paul says, "I am crucified with Christ: nevertheless I live; yet not I, but Christ lives in me..."

The pattern of crucifixion confirms we are expected to carry our cross (burdens, trappings and heartaches of the world systems), like Christ. Like Christ, it is a certainty we will suffer loss and pain as we reject and denounce the world systems (culture/matrix). And, like Christ, when we arrive at the end of pursuing our fleshly desires and agenda, we commit ourselves (our spirit) into the hands of the Father. As committed slaves of Christ, this is the pattern and process for submitting to His Lordship. The crux of being crucified with Christ is we desire to come to the end of our selfish will and desires (we desire to end our homage to self/flesh) and we commit our spirit (the entirety of our being) into the Lordship of Christ.

Our heart cries out to Jesus, "Into your hands, I commit my spirit."

When we solely depend on Christ it becomes apparent because we "die" to the world system (the sinful matrix); while we're obviously still in the world, it ceases to carry weight or significance. Romans 6:11 puts it this way, "In the same way, count yourselves dead to sin but alive to God in Christ Jesus." According to Galatians 5:24, "Those who belong to Christ Jesus have crucified the flesh with its passions and desires." A crucified life is a life wholly dependent on Jesus. Jesus is the only way. He, alone, provides the will and capacity to overcome the world system. The crucified life is the life I witnessed being lived through my friends and mentors Larry and Dean; incredible men, living as wonderful examples.

LIFE WITH JESUS

The tradition of making a partial commitment to the Lord (for instance, accepting Jesus as Savior, but not Lord) misses the point. Biblically, there is no such thing. If Jesus is not Lord of all (the entirety of our life, inclusive of all domains), He cannot be Lord at all! When we sincerely commit to follow Jesus, we are pledging our whole life. Jesus is all-sufficient and more than enough, so submission to His divine authority is to be holistically overlaid onto every area of life. The desire to be a servant to Jesus (as insurance against hell) but rejecting the sanctification process required to become a willing slave yoked to Him is admitting the desire to remain entangled as a slave to lies, deceptions, and oppression of the world system. Joining the "body," but not the "head" (Jesus/Lordship) prevents partaking in the freedom and abundance Jesus promises. That said, most Christians sincerely believe their conversion and spiritual formation experience is demonstrative of both servant and slave of Jesus. Alas, they are deceived. With chaos rampaging within the body of Christ (i.e., immorality, racism, "deconstructing faith," etc.), it is obvious that the Lordship is not represented and understood.

Those who assert "the body of Christ is doing fine" and believe the Lordship of Christ is already fully apparent in the current state of churches would have to believe Jesus is double-minded and willingly ceding His authority in deference to rampant secularism/demonism within culture. God forbid! The Church is experiencing too many fractious factions and strident divisions, causing caustic disunity throughout the church body. Churches today experience disunity based on race/ethnicity grievances, political agitation, sex/gender grievances, "power trips," and myriad culturally addictive trappings that dominate church messaging and function.

If we overwhelmingly confirm and practice submission to the Lordship of Jesus, wouldn't we see more unity and less grievance and bitterness within His church body? Wouldn't we see more marriage purity and less divorce? Wouldn't there by more cultural unity and less racial strife? Wouldn't we see less accommodation for manifest evils like abortion, sexual immorality and Marxist schemes like "social justice" (the acceptance of "other gospels")? How can so many claim to have inherited salvation as servant of God and slave to Christ while being gripped and swept into cultural trends designed to accommodate raging demonism? The evidence is clear and quite convicting. We have yet to fully comprehend and attain the grace of enjoying being freed to become both servant and slave to Jesus.

DESPERATE TIMES DEMAND DESPERATE MEASURES

We are desperate. We are human beings desperately in need of Jesus as Savior and Lord/Master. This is the most significant revelation of Jesus when attempting to break the chains of secular bondage. The revelation and relationship that comports with being yoked to the Master assures the life we expect in God's Kingdom. He promises us freedom and rest and He cannot lie or break a promise. If we neglect to embrace Lordship, we abdicate Jesus' command and empower the world system to continue our enslavement to the demonic realm replete with cultural mindsets designed to perpetually ensnare and defile. The old self must "die" and be truly born again. Our spirit must be reborn!

John 3:1-6 confirms it this way, "Now there was a man of the Pharisees named Nicodemus, a ruler of the Jews. This man came to Jesus by night and said to him, 'Rabbi, we know that you are a teacher come from God, for no one can do these signs that you do unless God is with him. 'Jesus answered him, 'Truly, truly, I say to you, unless one is born again he cannot see the kingdom of God.' Nicodemus said to him, 'How can a man be born when he is old? Can he enter a second time into his mother's womb and be born?' Jesus answered, 'Truly, truly, I say to you, unless one is born of water and the Spirit, he cannot enter the kingdom of God. That which is born of the flesh is flesh, and that which is born of the Spirit is spirit.'" Jesus confirms that the act of being born again is mandated if we desire to overcome the flesh. Our flesh is inextricably tied to the world system, and this means it must endure the process of death and rebirth.

Sincere commitment to spiritual formation submitted under the Lordship of Christ requires that we come to the "end" of ourselves. Our "end" is the beginning! The flesh holds the unspiritual mind and body that bows in submission to bondage and oppression of the world system. It is the container of sinful desires and impulses that prevents us from obeying God's spiritual laws. In Christ, we present our members—bodies, minds, will, etc.—as slaves in the service of righteousness. We should do this with the same zeal that we once had as slaves to bondage and oppression of the world system. Our old self operated out of the fulfilling lust and pride of the flesh, which has been "sold under sin." Our new identity, as a slave to Christ, has been imputed unto righteousness. Righteous living is the new beginning.

Beginning anew as a slave to Jesus means we are willing to endure a similar pattern of death. While it may sound ironic that we must die in order to live in Christ, considering we are born into a world that is the polar opposite of the world God promises, having to die to that world to live in a new world (and Kingdom) makes total sense. Jesus' pattern of crucifixion and death confirms the pathway for how we are reborn and set free to a new life in His Kingdom!

FIRST (IN THE KINGDOM) IS THE SLAVE!

There is an often overlooked or misunderstood distinction between the nuanced dichotomy of the commitment to become a servant of Jesus and a slave of Jesus. Since the distinction is nuanced, it's easy to miss altogether. One accepts Jesus as Savior to receive blessings in eternity. The other recognizes the dearth of meaning and vanity of the world and declares a vital need for Him as Savior and Lord. The latter is the "first." Jesus

Himself makes the distinction clear by distinguishing between "great" and "first." In Matthew 20:26-27, Jesus says, "It shall not be so among you. But whoever would be great among you must be your servant, and whoever would be first among you must be your slave." In these verses, Jesus is challenging the conventional understanding of leadership and greatness prevalent in the world. While many try to collapse the domains of servant and slave (by asserting when you commit to serving Christ, it implies you're a servant and slave), but there is a distinction between servant and slave, and Jesus demands a specific commitment to both.

When Jesus talks about being a servant and slave, He confirms the route to number one status in His Kingdom comes through becoming a slave. A servant agrees to meet a certain standard, and meet the needs of others in exchange for money, an act of friendship, or in this case a promise for eternity in Heaven. But a slave typically acts under compulsion (personal volition) or obligation with no expectation of recompense. That said, "slave" is distinguished as a having deeper level of self-sacrifice and obedience. A slave is not only serving but doing so with complete submission to the needs and wishes of others (in this case the Lord). Jesus describes greatness in His Kingdom as belonging to those who serve others, but the very top spot belongs to those who commit to living as a slave to Him.

Understanding how God differentiates between a servant and a slave in His Kingdom helps illuminate why current discord persists within the body of Christ (the church). Generally speaking, churches are led by those who have a focus on making a commitment to servanthood, but oftentimes, these same individuals are trapped and enslaved by prevailing currents/ trends within culture. They don't commit to Lordship (of Christ), therefore the toxic culture consumes them to the point their lord and master is still the fallen world – the matrix.

The old axiom (actually drawn from the Bible) that "you can't serve two masters," rings true. It is impossible to serve the master of the world system/matrix, and the Master of God's Kingdom at the same time; one always takes precedence over the other. This means being tethered, even in the least bit, to the momentum of change within the (demonically inspired) cultural tide produces a change in mindset and perspective. Often, the ebbs and flows of changing cultural tides drive actions and intents antithetical to the Gospel. Grotesque heresies and wholly immoral "carnal Christians" multiply instead of a Kingdom culture. What we commonly refer to as "backsliding" is a direct result of the attempt to hold to two masters. On one hand, there is a marginal commitment as servant to Jesus, but the strongholds and tether to the seductions in culture consumes actions and intents leading to failure in a principled Christian commitment. This is the syndrome (vacillating between masters) dominating parishioners and clergy/ministry leaders suffering with continued bondages and oppression of the world. Without commitment to the Lordship of Christ (rejections of world system, then crucified with Christ, death to self, rebirth into Spirit of righteousness) many will endure perpetual cycles of failure and defeat.

FAILURE OF FALLACIOUS FALSITIES

Presented as attempts to remain culturally relevant, a spread of heresies and "other gospels" in the form of neo-Marxist proclamations are intoned while being preached over the pulpit. Dysfunction, disunity, and disorder are the fruits produced by this trend. The Church will continue to be marginally effective and impotent until it fully embodies a commitment to embrace being yoked (enslaved) under the authority of Jesus. His Lordship! Sadly, until this shift happens, prevailing dysfunction will continue to cast a "dim light" in the world instead of the glorious light reflective of a shining beacon of hope Jesus intends.

The spread of false doctrines and a general lack of knowledge has prompted many to commit as a servant of God awaiting eternal salvation, but unwittingly reject becoming slaves to Jesus. To be sure, there is rampant loathing, dissension and hate within the church. A slave to Jesus cannot hate! A slave to Jesus does not spread condemnation toward others within the body of Christ! A slave to Jesus doesn't partake in satan's work as "accuser of the brethren," as they accuse vast numbers of their fellow Christians. When we observe Clergy and/or parishioners partaking in the castigating of others by accusing them using sophomoric cultural tropes such as "White Christian Nationalism," it is evidence they are bound as a slave to culture, not Jesus. Through the example of their lives, Larry and Dean confirmed to me that a servant of Jesus refrains from such actions because complete commitment to the Lordship of Christ defines the life of a slave to Jesus. Such a slave lives with the motto, "I have come to my end, and into your hands (Jesus) I commit my spirit!"

The good news is, we will flourish and fulfill all God intended when "death" comes to life!

Six

Life After Death:
"Life" begins with death...
Death begins rebirth....

"**I**s it dead? Or has it become so convoluted and overlaid with complexities that it doesn't function?" This was the question I had to address when a family member sought my recommendation for a new computer, printer, and peripherals after their entire system suddenly stopped working. Given my extensive experience in information technology spanning decades, I often receive such calls from friends and family.

Suspecting an underlying issue beyond a complete system failure, I embarked on diagnosing the computer systems. It became apparent that the problem lay in the chaotic arrangement of wires, extension cords, and outdated peripherals connected to... nothing! The mass of complexity and clutter took hours to untangle. After streamlining the setup, I reverted to the basic connections: the computer directly to the power source, the printer to the computer, and discarded all the outdated and irrelevant peripherals. Ultimately, the issue stemmed from decades of layered, convoluted technologies disrupting the simplicity of the "computer and printer" connection.

This scenario of renewing the "simple connection" to the original source, akin to the computer and printer, is what appears to be missing within Christendom. While numerous sermons and messages have captivated by providing temporary edification and hope, they have, at times, complicated the fundamental truth of the importance of being yoked to Jesus and His Lordship. Trending messages that intone "name it and claim it," "prosperity," "living a purpose-driven life," "living your best life," and "...thou art loosed" (just to name a few) have inspired many but have also contributed to the convolution of the simple truth that all these aspirations are simply found in Him (Yeshua). Once embraced, these trends have cluttered, cascaded, and overlaid our biblical understanding to the point where the straightforward connection to our essential source for everything we need has rendered the Lordship of Christ seemingly intricate and convoluted. The truth is, it's not that complicated. The message and pathway remain simple— activation through a direct connection to His Lordship.

The pursuit of Lordship demands following the pattern of Jesus. Again, this means we will "carry the cross" (meaning all the trappings of bondage and oppression of the world system), and we will be "crucified" by laying down our life and its foundation's rooted in lust, pride, and bondages (these are most prevalent in the quest to accommodate our five senses). When we come to the end of ourselves, we fully surrender by embracing Jesus' last words, "'Father, into your hands I commit my spirit"; this indicates a heart of total surrender into His Lordship. Then, and only then, does the rebirth into a life of abundance begins.

Under the Lordship of Jesus, we are promised to live in life in abundance (whole and complete without lack in any domain). Jesus says, "The thief comes only in order to steal and kill and destroy. I came that they may have life, and have it in abundance [to the full, till it overflows]" (John 10:10 AMP). Jesus confirmed the world system is designed to be infused with bondage enabled by our foe's (satan's) desire to steal, kill, and destroy us. Jesus came to overcome the fallen world by giving us His Kingdom, which provides life eternal and life in abundance (to the full and overflowing). This promise is for those who are crucified with Christ and born again into His character and likeness. Most grapple with the process of laying down our lives; it's in our nature to accommodate the five senses (and fickle emotions attached to them). They are thoroughly entangled with the world system, making rebirth in Christ almost impossible. Exactly how does this work?

NEWLEY CREATED "NEW CREATION!"

2 Corinthians 5:14-18 illuminates how to become a new creation in Christ (under His Lordship). It reads, "For Christ's *love compels* us, because we are convinced that one died for all, and therefore *all died*. And he died for all, that those who live should *no longer live for themselves* but for him who died for them and was raised again. So, from now on, *we regard no one from a worldly point of view*. Though we once regarded

Christ in this way, we do so no longer. Therefore, if *anyone is in Christ, the new creation has come*: The old has gone, the new is here! All this is from God, who reconciled us to Himself through Christ and gave us the ministry of reconciliation." Wow! This message is potent with rich and profound Biblical wisdom and truth. It confirms how to traverse the incredible pathway from death (bondage), transcending the fallen world, into life (new birth in Christ); the individual transformation and its outcomes for humanity are remarkably clarified through this passage.

2 Corinthians 5 confirms the following process and pathway for becoming a new creation in Christ Jesus. First, it confirms we are compelled to His Lordship because of our love for Him; this is a decision that comes out of the volition of our heart, not duress. We don't view becoming a slave to Jesus as arduous and problematic; we do it because of a deep and abiding love for Him. We willingly submit to His authority and want to make Him master because we fully understand that if He isn't our master, the unrelenting world system is. This binary choice defines our purposeful commitment to Him.

Secondly, 2 Corinthians 5 confirms the process of following His pattern means we must "die" because He died for all. In this context, we experience death to this worldly system. We desire to make a commitment to die to self; therefore, we no longer live guided by our selfish/fleshly motivations or inclinations (guided by our five senses and unbridled emotions). Death to self and the world system is vital because that system is led and guided by another master (our foe, satan) and is designed to ensnare us with bondages laden with trappings designed steal, kill, and destroy us. The world system must be cast off; to do so, we bow under the Lordship of Christ and, with our new Master, we definitively reject participating in it any longer.

One of the most critical yet easily ignored points of 2 Corinthians is that the precursor to becoming a new creation is that we *no longer regard anyone from a worldly point of view.* This is powerful yet problematic! It is powerful because it confirms that in order to be a new creation man, *all* old memories, imaginations, triggers, faults, unforgiveness, and virtually everything that held us in bondage are to be no longer regarded (they hold no "weight" or authority going forward). When we are born anew, we can't have the weight of the past cast forward in our new life. It is inconceivable for a "new creation" to be dogged, triggered, and manipulated by things of the past. (For people suffering from anxiety and depression, past things plant traps and triggers; embracing the new birth in Christ moves us away from all those past things and toward a new life.)

A new creation is just that. It's new! Think about it: a newborn baby can't know anything; everything is learned anew from its birth. The same is true with becoming a new creation and being rebirthed in Christ. If we are newly created, there can be no regard for the world (including worldly ideologies and perspectives) and the past (including unmet expectations/ wants, hurts, and dreams); all are left behind and forgotten. This allows us to regard everyone in a new light. (I pray you are getting this truth because the embodiment of this truth is truly life-changing!) Having no regard for the past is the crucible of what brings us into a life of abundance in Christ. The single most evident "thorn" in the side of Christians and clergy is we have extreme difficulty letting go of the past. It almost seems that we find pleasure holding the past (past failures, guilt, shame etc.) over the heads of others.

Would Critical Race Theory (CRT) resonate in the hearts and minds of Christians/and clergy if we had *no regard for the past*? Think about it. CRT advances that all whites are complicit with chattel slavery (American slave trade) that ended over 160 years ago. Would there be a demand for reparations if there were no regard to hold others accountable for wretched actions of the past? Would demands for DEI (Diversity, Equity, Inclusion) persist if there were no regard for the past? Would Liberation Theology/Black Liberation theology trend upwards if there were no regard for the past?

When we regard the past as preeminent, we render the Cross impotent. When we regard the past, we imply Jesus is insufficient. We imply Jesus cannot appropriately handle meting out justice and/or vengeance. We demand that the need for immediate gratification (whereby some identified foes suffer right now) is paramount, therefore reliance on Cross and Jesus must subordinate to our grotesque emotions. GOD FORBID! Anyone who continues to hold grudges against others with full regard for the past (driven by ruminations, resentments, etc.) confirms they are not a "new creation," not an ambassador for Christ, and not submitted under the Lordship of Christ. Only sincere repentance and adoption of a heart that forgives can mitigate these heretical imaginations!

Only by undergoing the process of becoming a new creation through *repentance* (broken and contrite about the past) and *forgiveness* (possessing a heart that forgives for the past and present) can one arrive to the point at having no regard for the past. Our enemy (satan) knows we will be forever haunted by our past (our hurts, shame, guilt, etc.) if forgiveness is not extended. He knows he can keep us tethered to his arcane ecosystems of bondage and oppression if we continue to be dogged and dragged by ruminations of the past. Grudgingly, we must admit that holding onto the past and unforgiveness are the "Achilles heel" for many followers of Christ. Many "think" they are "new creations" and ambassadors of reconciliation, but in truth, they don't qualify because of their unwillingness to let go of aspects of the world system that have them gripped and bound.

Becoming a new creation and ambassador of reconciliation, as described in 2 Corinthians, comes by way of an exclusive pathway. This pathway isn't easier or less discriminatory for pastors/clergy or anyone else; the pathway places a demand on the fundamental tenet of becoming a new creation via strict obedience from everyone who desires to become an ambassador of reconciliation!

The fundamental requirement that we have no regard for the past doesn't mean we "forgive and forget." It doesn't make one a "chump" or push-over. It simply means we do not carry the weight of our memories and are no longer driven (emotionally) by our past. It means, going forward, we are committed to only being driven and inspired by our Master. Notably, this (no regard for the past) provides answers to why there is so much disunity and inner-church strife and discord dominating the church experience today. Too many are manipulated and controlled by false narratives in culture (the matrix) to the point they are precluded from taking a posture of forgiveness.

Consider this: Would churches experience dysfunctional, distrusting, and chaotic inner-denominational/inner-church strife if all participants had no regard for past hurts, guilt, or shame? Would divorce, sexual immorality, and countless other issues demonstrative of the world system continue to rampage within the church if clergy and parishioners were in full embrace of 2 Corinthians 5? This passage holds the key to our "death," rebirth, and resurrection in Christ as an ambassador.

A HEART THAT FORGIVES

Many Christians do not enjoy the abundant life promised by Jesus, and instead live a life of perpetual bondage, despair, and suffering. Even after accepting Christ, many feel there has been little or no change to the level of bondage and suffering they endure. Why? It may sound ironic and counter-intuitive, but our suffering ends when forgiveness begins! The biggest impediment to living a crucified life as a new creation in Christ revolves around the issue of forgiveness. Forgiveness is one of the most fundamental tenets of Christianity, yet it is often ignored or overlooked. Yet our ability to forgive is the principal function that helps set us free.

The amount of bondage and suffering many Christians endure are a by-product of the world system; "the matrix" is infused with instruments of manipulation and control, so an embrace of perpetual bitterness and aggrievement is a natural by-product and common attribute. Becoming "spiritually hardened" and insensitive (to the prompting of the Spirit) due to the amount of distress and hate promulgated via the world system can easily undermine spiritual formation. This is our plight, but there is an answer: We escape the world system and all its appendages through reliance on Christ as He commands the act of forgiveness.

Many passages in the Bible confirm we are to be in this world but not of it. Jesus' prayer in John 17 confirms, "Now I am no longer in the world, but these are in the world . . . They are not of the world, just as I am not of the world" (vv. 11, 16). In the book of John alone, Jesus refers to "the world" nineteen times! Jesus opens and ends His prayer, confessing that He transcends the world; therefore, we must do so as well. Based on the clear distinction that the world system is designed to enslave and abuse mankind with perpetual bondage and oppression, we should now be quite aware of the severity of Jesus' prayer and admonition that we transcend the world system. It's demonically inspired and infused with lies and deceptions, therefore, the antithesis of Christian life. The world system is purposely designed to keep mankind controlled and entrapped. A fundamental requisite is the need to transcend the horrors of our past and escape the world system (and all its tentacles) through a sincere heart embracing forgiveness!

Offering forgiveness after realizing the depth of countless ways humans endure horrible abuse (by former spouses, employers, lifestyle choices, etc.) can be extremely difficult. For some, the act of forgiveness is the most difficult thing to consider – sometimes it seems virtually impossible. Let's remember, however, that God would not command us to do what is impossible. If we perceive it as impossible (in our own strength), then we are to give it to Him. Said differently, if we earnestly confess to our Master that we feel we cannot forgive (for whatever reason or rationale), our loving Father, Master, and Friend understands, and He will give us the capacity to do it. (It may not come overnight, but ultimately, God gives us the capacity to sincerely forgive). Irrespective of the level of oppression and abuse, possessing a heart that forgives is not optional; it is mandated!

Our Master wants us to know that harboring unforgiveness may feel good at times (in our flesh), but it is a very high price to pay when compared to living a life tethered to the perpetual bondage of the world system. Unforgiveness even presents the risk of losing our eternal destiny. Matthew 18:21-35, Jesus provides a parable about the significance and severity of forgiveness. He confirms the application of forgiveness with the parable of the unmerciful servant as follows, "Then Peter came to Jesus and asked, 'Lord, how many times shall I forgive my brother or sister who sins against me? Up to seven times?' Jesus answered, 'I tell you, not seven times, but seventy-seven times. Therefore, the kingdom of heaven is like a king who wanted to settle accounts with his servants. As he began the settlement, a man who owed him ten thousand bags of gold was brought to him. Since he was not able to pay, the master ordered that he and his wife and his children and all that he had be sold to repay the debt. At this the servant fell on his knees before him. 'Be patient with me,' he begged, 'and I will pay back everything. The servant's master took pity on him, canceled the debt and let him go. But when that servant went out, he found one of his fellow servants who owed him a hundred silver coins. He grabbed him and began to choke him. 'Pay back what you owe me!' he demanded. His fellow servant fell to his knees and begged him, 'Be patient with me, and I will pay it back.' But he refused. Instead, he went off and had the man thrown into prison until he could pay the debt. When the other servants saw what had happened, they were outraged and went and told their master everything that had happened. Then the master called the servant in. 'You wicked servant,' he said, 'I canceled all that debt of yours because you begged me to. Shouldn't you have had mercy on your fellow servant just as I had on you?' In anger his master handed him over to the jailers to be tortured, until he should pay back all he owed. This is how my heavenly Father will treat each of you unless you forgive your brother or sister from your heart.'" We can see from this parable that our Master wants us to thoroughly understand that He already paid the ultimate price for us and now shows us mercy by forgiving *all* we have done! With His incredible act to forgive us of all sins, He provides the expectation for forgiveness we are to extend (following His pattern) for others. Therefore, it should be obvious that forgiveness is a command we must comply with accordingly (albeit very difficult for some); forgiveness is not optional!

In stubbornness, unforgiveness is the crux of what keeps humanity tethered and exposed to unrelenting attacks from the world system. Unforgiveness is a significant impediment that endangers our life in this realm and is also an existential threat to our eternal souls. While many may feel holding grievances and bitterness against others is, in some instances, an appropriate response, the Word of God confirms it is not. Several Bible passages provide confirmation of how slaves to Christ are to mitigate feelings of perpetual grievance and unforgiveness:

- "Bearing with one another and, if one has a complaint against another, *forgiving each other; as the Lord has forgiven you, you must also forgive*"(Col. 3:13).
- "Judge not, and you will not be judged; condemn not, and you will not be condemned; *forgive, and you will be forgiven*"(Luke 6:37).
- "And whenever you stand praying, *forgive* if you have anything against anyone, so that your Father also who is in heaven may *forgive* you your trespasses. But if you do not *forgive*, neither will your Father in heaven *forgive* your transgressions" (Mark 11:25-26 and Matt 6:14-15).

Forgiveness is a command, and God's Word demands it as an unequivocal act of obedience. It also confirms the inconvenient truth that if we don't forgive, our Father in heaven will not forgive us. Ouch! Really? Why? The clearest reason why forgiveness is required is based on Jesus' parable. If He forgives us for any and everything, it is audacious and with great pride, hubris and arrogance that we decline to forgive others (pride, in any form, is anathema to God). The act of obedience to God's command to forgive provides the tell-tell sign of whether someone is freed as a servant and slave to Christ or still suffering from the bondage and oppression of the world system.

A person who is sincerely crucified with Christ and experienced rebirth as a new creation is marked by a heart that forgives. Those who do not possess a heart that forgives, are marked by constantly ranting and raving about being victimized based on unfairness and "inequities" suffer from the bondage of the world system. Forgiveness provides freedom by breaking bonds of hate, blame, guilt, etc., and this untethers us from the fallen world. *We are freed by truth, and the truth confirms we must forgive.* A crucified life culminates in the fundamental truth of need for repentance and sincere acts of forgiveness; this is what allows our Master to use us as His new creation.

IN ORDER TO LIVE UNFORGIVENESS MUST DIE!

Promised abundant living cannot begin until unforgiveness dies. The spirit of unforgiveness is rampaging and manifesting in all domains and realms. With God's mandate confirming that we must forgive, in a society where many stridently demand to hold to spirit of unforgiveness (via CRT, DEI, Social Justice, Black Liberation, Marxism, etc.), we are now witnessing the literal time period when the "wheat is separated from the chaff." Up to now, the wheat and chaff have grown and prospered together, but in this time and season, we are witnessing with our own eyes (and heart) a clear separation. Jesus proclaimed a (metaphorical) distinction between "goats" and "sheep" (Matthew 25:31-46), and we are now witnessing it.

Jesus describes how He will be separating people as a shepherd separates the sheep from the goats. He asserts the righteous (likened to sheep) since they hear His voice and follow Him; they are those who have repented and forgiven others and accepted all tenets of the Kingdom. The sheep inherit the Kingdom. Conversely, He asserts the unrighteous are the goats. These are those who are stubbornly hold to their own will, meander and pretend to be a part of His flock but are unshakably tethered to world system; these don't hear Jesus' voice commanding repentance and forgiveness, and instead possess hardened hearts of unforgiveness (and other evils). These (goats) will face the cruel reality of God's judgment.

When observing prevailing negative trends within the church, we are witnesses to Jesus' separation (of goats and sheep) in "real-time!" By the grace of God, we are provided the opportunity to witness a glorious revelation (distinction between goats and sheep), and unless there is a pronounced change within the church, many who purport to be "Christians" (followers of Christ, but in reality, are goats) will reap existential consequences.

The sad reality is that based on prevailing trends in Christendom, the church (generally) does not reflect "hearts that forgive" or "new creations" in Christ. I do not say this to be "judgmental"; regrettably, it is a matter of fact. The current "fruit" we discern as having a significant impact on the body of Christ includes trends toward: (1) "progressive Christianity";

(2) cultural syncretism' (3) condemning denominations or factions as "White Christian Nationalists" or "White Evangelicals"; (4) demands that Critical Race Theory (CRT) is a "gospel issue" and wholly necessary for Biblical living; (5) claiming "social justice" as a necessary issue for extra-biblical social activism; (6) asserting "reparations" as a necessary tenet for unity; and myriad other issues. Since we are admonished that we will "know them by their fruit," it is easy to discern the prevailing fruit within the church is rotten. It is defiled by the world system. Many clergy and ministry leaders are stubbornly aggrieved with bouts of bitterness and strife that steer them and their flocks away from having a broken and contrite heart willing to forgive. Offense, hate, bitterness and perpetual aggrievement feed the spirit of unforgiveness. The spirit of unforgiveness must die if we are to live!

Underlying evils running rampant within the culture are perpetual and insatiable grievances and indicative of unforgiveness (holding fast to victimhood; demanding retribution for something believed owed). As noted, these mindsets pose an existential threat to the soul. For example, mindsets holding that blacks were severely harmed/wronged by white people (the grievance) and therefore all white people are complicit cannot and will not be forgiven for it – means that the wrongs will never be remedied (the unforgiveness). Such mindsets are replete with the demonic influence of unforgiveness.

While God demands all His children adopt a heart that forgives, the world system drives narratives wholly antithetical to people of Faith by asserting unforgiveness is somehow appropriate at times (based on common themes of racism, sexism, genderism, etc.), and "enlightened" or Progressive. At the moment, the world system dominates these cultural arguments. If a heart that forgives were prevailing throughout the body of Christ, then these arcane secular (neo-Marxist) conversations would be deemed ridiculous, adolescent and sophomoric! They would be wholly irrelevant.

The cultural tide having a significant negative impact on the body of Christ surrounds the infusion of "other gospels" that the Apostle Paul warned about (Gal 1:8-9). New "theologies" like Black Liberation Theology (and Liberation Theology generally) consistently agitate on myriad race issues and the demand for "social action"/activism. Biblical truths that deal with dying to self, rejecting the world system, and becoming a new creation in Christ are completely ignored in deference to these "new" theological ideas. Since they are heavily inspired by insidious neo-Marxist/cultural Marxist ideologies, these "new" ideas fall well short of Jesus' teachings and Biblical commands, norms and standards.

No doubt, some of cultural Marxism's slogans and talking points seem seductively clever and may make some people feel good at some level. Any such good feeling is terribly temporary. Embracing cultural gospels that inflame race/grievance and exacerbate unforgiveness means an eternal death sentence for the soul. People who imbibe these other gospels and hold these reprobate mindsets confirm their continued embrace of the world system, which leads to unequivocal and definitive consequences.

The fact is, man cannot serve two masters. This world has two kingdoms at war (Kingdom of God ("good") vs. kingdom of darkness ("evil")). It has two masters at war (King Jesus vs. "god of this world" satan). It has two diametrically opposed languages (Jesus speaks *truth* vs. *lies* with satan the father of lies). And it has two polar opposite living standards (Jesus' truth sets us free vs. satan's lies providing perpetual bondage). We can and must decide to love one and hate the other! Matthew 6:24-26 says it this way, "No man can serve two masters: for either he will hate the one, and love the other; or else he will hold to the one, and despise the other..." We have the freedom to choose which kingdom and master, so what is your decision?

OBLIGED TO OBLIVIOUS OBLIVION

The bulk of humanity seems oblivious to the existential battle for the soul. I have found the battle becomes clearer when we arrive at the point when we can distinguish the unrelenting impact of the matrix as it encircles humanity with tentacles that bind humanity to the things of this world. When we begin to see and distinguish the world with a God-view lens, we can take steps to become the new creation God desires. The oblivious becomes obvious! Then, truth can begin its work to set us free.

Fundamental truths call upon us to *love one another* (1 John 4:11) and *forgive one another* (Eph. 4:31-32). If we love one another and forgive one another, we would not have "race issues" impacting the quest toward unity in churches and denominations. Moreover, the all agitation, bitterness, and hatred we attribute to purported race disparities are already dispelled because *Jesus broke all the barriers between "races," and we are one in Christ* (Eph 2:14-16). This truth makes it possible to sincerely extend love and forgiveness toward one another (irrespective of race, denomination, or culture). The truth is, Jesus already reconciled all races; this means there is literally no need for racial reconciliation, instead, we need *racial restoration*.

We need to be restored to the truth that acknowledges our Master has already fully reconciled us to Himself as one body. If we accept that we are a new creation (meaning we have no regard for the past, we are repentant, and embrace a heart that forgives), we have been truly set free! Jesus provided a permanent "fix" to all the many other cultural issues facing the church as well. He counsels against trends in humanity toward complicit obliviousness so we can receive a full embrace of His love and forgiveness in every domain. We can escape the matrix, but we must reject oblivion to accept the obviousness of Jesus as Master.

FREED TO BE SERVANT AND SLAVE TO JESUS

As we survey our current times, it becomes evident that the world is ensnared in a spell – a spell cast by witchcraft. Witchcraft, in essence, is intertwined with demonism, permeating the entire ecosystem of lies and deceit. This intricate web of deception is crafted with entanglements that give rise to bondage and oppression. Stemming from the fall of man in the Garden of Eden, this is the pervasive environment into which everyone is born, automatically subjecting them to enslavement. Humanity finds itself entangled in a world system meticulously designed to steal, kill, and destroy. Though the overwhelming weight of this reality is palpable, there exists an avenue of escape from the clutches of this wretched enslavement orchestrated by humanity's adversary, satan. This escape is the only alternative choice available.

God has awesomely provided a way to escape being enslaved to the otherwise inescapable sin of the world system. He provided His Son Yeshua (Jesus). Jesus was born, died, and was resurrected to conquer the bondage of the world system and provide an alternative system offering true freedom. With mankind having to make a binary choice of either being a slave to sin and the world system, or being set free from this world system through becoming a slave unto righteousness, a choice for Yeshua is choosing to be set free from the bondage and oppressions of the world system. It is the only alternative and escape from the lies and trappings of the world system.

Making a choice to escape the world system requires that we not only choose to become a servant of Jesus by accepting Him as our Savior but also that we are yoked to Him (as co-laborers) as a *slave*. Unlike the world system and our preconceived notions of slavery, this form of enslavement comes as a choice that is made out of the volition of the soul, not out of coercion or threat. We choose to become enslaved (unto righteousness) because of our love and compulsion toward Yeshua. By our dutifully committing to His yoke, He deems us greater than the greatest and "first" among many in His Kingdom. This is tremendous because not only are we made first, but we finally sever our tether to the perpetual bondage and oppression of the world system. We are set free with His yoke!

The process of becoming yoked to Jesus requires we follow His pattern of death and resurrection. Jesus' death was through crucifixion; likewise, (euphemistically) we are to "carry our cross" and be "crucified with Christ." With his last breaths, Jesus said, "Father, into your hands I commit my spirit." With the same abandon, we are to follow His pattern and leave behind the trappings of this world by also declaring, "Father, into your hands I commit my spirit" (meaning, I am yours, O God, I yield complete control of my life in submission to You). This begins the process of severing ties to the world system. Then comes our resurrection.

Jesus died and, on the third day, was resurrected. Likewise, when we abandon ourselves to our Lord and commit to dying to this world system, we are rebirthed as a new creation. The biggest condition of actually receiving a new beginning is that we have no regard for our past life (just like a newborn child learns from his parents, we are born ready to learn from our Master anew without the trappings of our past). This means we give no weight, glory, or motivation to our past. It is no longer a "driver" for any ideas, decisions, or actions because we are indeed a new birth in Christ Jesus! We understand that taking any actions due to considerations manufactured by the old self are trappings and bondage. That said, we put on the mind of Christ and move forward as a vessel of His glory. This is evidenced when we are no longer triggered (moved in any way) by racial strife/divisions, hate/rage, covetousness and jealousies, and all forms of immortality; those feelings and attitudes are swept away, no longer credited against us as "new creations" in Christ.

Not all have understood and transitioned into a new creation. Many are stuck with the mindset of a servant awaiting recompense of Heaven while tethered to the world system. We realize this is not what God intended and this realization helps keep us humble and prayerful for our brothers and sisters struggling inside this "cycle of death." We see that many clergy and ministers are hurting, still suffering from issues of the past (historical hurts and unmet expectations) and are aggrieved and oppressed by issues involving race/ethnicity, covetousness, and guilt and shame. Their struggles are apparent as they point fingers of condemnation while demanding reparations, social justice, or any number of other culturally divined schemes. We sincerely and earnestly pray for these people because (regardless of their title or role) they have not become a new creation. It's evidenced by their continued harboring of a heart of unforgiveness, and we recognize this as an existential threat to their souls. So, we pray that Lordship takes root and reigns!

Many Christians have professed Jesus as Savior but do not necessarily embrace Him as Lord. Irrespective of what they proclaim, the truth is, either Jesus is Lord of all, or He's not Lord at all! There is no such thing as a partial acceptance of Jesus. Since humanity cannot escape enslavement, and it is a binary decision, those who accept Jesus as Savior but decline Lordship are wholly accepting to remain enslaved by the world system; sadly, they remain susceptible to all its tentacles and trappings of bondage and destruction. We must sincerely pray for people as their soul is tethered to a world of sin, and they continue to endure undue suffering as a result. We pray they accept the truth of Jesus' Lordship, the need for repentance, and the command to forgive. When they come to know this truth, they will indeed be set free!

Based on the foundations and fundamentals of what was discovered about the world system grounded in lies, deceptions, and bondage, versus being set free through Christ (the way, truth, and life), old deceptive narratives about the "sacred-secular divide" should not exist. There should be no such thing as "woke" pastors, progressive Christianity, syncretism, and Liberation theologists! These are not only anathemas to the Gospel and an affront to the Lordship of Christ, they are diabolical schemes specifically created undermine people of Faith so they remain tethered to systems of bondage and oppression.

Notably, the whole insidious idea of the "sacred-secular divide" that refers to a distinct separation between "faith" aspects of life (the sacred) and non-religious or worldly aspects (the secular), has exacerbated humanity's current plight. People who hold to this "divide" idea so they can continue holding to the bondage of the world system while also asserting Christianity. This is a damnable heresy, as it tries to mix "the sacred with the profane." With this diabolical scheme, our foe has proffered a concept that influences people to demarcate domains of their lives in order to comfortably move between different spheres (even if those spheres are in conflict or are diametrically hypocritical to other domains). This often leads to a subtle creeping and integration of the secular realms (the world system and all its appendages) taking over (most if not all) aspects of life; our foe entices by making the matrix seductive and compelling. Ultimately, a collapse of life's domains and convergence takes place. This is what precipitates the "backsliding" trend; this vicious cycle only adds bondage and suffering while elongating enslavement to the world system.

A clear example of the "sacred/secular" divide appears when we vote. In nations where people can vote (representative democracies), we can witness Christians being conflicted in relation to "sacred/secular." Voting creates an arena where Christian consternation is most prevalent. Christians (through the lust and power of the world system) feel they can vote for whomever (and for whatever reasons) they want; voting is seen as part of an individual's freedom right? Uh, not so under the Lordship of Christ! When under Lordship, "fleshly" predilections driven by our unprincipled and fickle emotions go away. (Remember, new creations give *no regard for the* past, and this includes memories or traditions of our favored political party). Under the Lordship of Christ, we (by definition) have no emotional tie to any party. We pray for discernment and just cast a vote based on alignment with God's Word, and let the chips fall wherever they may.

Based on the frothing fervency of some who delight in persecuting and holding disdain toward others for just having differing political opinions (done mostly by "Progressives"), it almost seems some have erected political altars to be worshipped in "Christian" households. Cherishing and relying on political affiliation (and associated party, "personalities," ethnicity, sex/gender, etc.) to make voting decisions, as opposed to strict reliance on the Lord/Master and His Word, amounts to willful acts of reprobation and dereliction! An acute level of cognitive dissonance manifests fully when "woke" types express audacious indignation as they proudly preen "Progressive" while mandating everyone vote for anti-Christ politicians and policies. Again, only those who hold to insidious "sacred-secular divide" mindsets can somehow do the mental gymnastics needed to reconcile their actions and voting patterns. This is a tell-tale sign of a soul lacking Lordship with Christ. These people are still woefully entangled in the matrix of the world system and need deliverance. When we recognize them, we should encourage them to God's standard of "forgiveness" and encourage them that we are praying for their full deliverance (from the world).

Voting illustrates clearly how people can be trapped and in bondage to the sacred-secular divide. When it comes to participating in the domain of voting, it seems that many Christians idolize and worship their favored party rather than the Lord. This divide is most obvious when Christians seem all too happy to vote in lock-step with demonic secularists based on their family tradition. It is also recognizable when we observe people of faith giving homage to wretched political party policies and ideologies (policies literally designed to assault and undermine Faith) without any consideration of the need to not lean to their own understanding and instead strictly rely on the Word of God (voting only for those "more closely aligned" with it) as the guide.

Often, "mega Pastors" and "Bishops" use their respective influence (and pulpits) to proudly honor and encourage their favorite party and politician even as they (the politicians) represent virtually everything that God detests! They (pastors/clergy) do this without any sense of shame or need for repentance. The sacred-secular divide is a purposeful lie developed by our foe to keep us manipulated, controlled and tethered to his evil kingdom and under the bondage of his authority. Make no mistake, those who participate in the aforementioned ways have not become a new creation and have not yet accepted Jesus as Lord (by definition)! Again, either Yeshua is Lord of all (every domain of life), or He's not Lord at all! We sincerely pray for these many souls entrapped by an unforgiving heart.

While issues of race and voting patterns are just two examples representing some of the significant cultural influences on the church, there are countless ways that indicate whether we are tethered to the world (governed by master satan) or wholly submitted under the Lordship of Christ (ruled by the Master Jesus). Cries for reparations, condemnation of "White Christian Nationalists/Evangelicals," assertions that all whites are complicit in racism (i.e., tropes developed out of CRT/DEI), sexual deviancy and immorality, preaching syncretism (melding the demonic culture with the purity of the Gospel message) and a "progressive/woke" gospel form just the tip of the proverbial iceberg. These open and obvious examples should be relevant to help appropriately discern and distinguish between competing dichotomies in which we have the freedom to choose to participate. Servants and slaves to Jesus must realize there are countless cultural fiefdoms that must end. The only way to permanently end them requires sincerely becoming a new creation (again, "no regard for the past") and submitting to the Lordship of Christ.

The choice is simple! We can choose to disobediently hold fast to unforgiveness while continuing to be tethered to the matrix of the world system made up of lies, deceit, and bondage therein. Or, we can choose to forgive, become a new creation, and be yoked to Master Jesus in order to be set free from all bondage.

Remember, a slave must be willing to leave where they are now, and follow the leading of the Master (Yeshua)! They will go places and submit to things never contemplated. They will demonstrate complete surrender. In order to live the glorious destiny God designed, Lordship is an inescapable necessity. The moment we say "NO," is the moment we dismiss Jesus as Lord. Lordship demands obedience 100%; partial obedience is disobedience and rebellion! "Progressive Christianity" is death, and it must end to make way for life in Christ to begin.

Again, life (real life) begins after death (death to "self" and death to the cultural matrix and all it appendages/bondages).

The good news is we are free to be obedient to God this day and choose our Master and Lord. Today we are free to accept being a servant of Christ and slave to Christ. We are freed to become Yeshua's servants. We are freed to become His slaves. We are freed to choose to holistically accept the fullness of His promises of freedom and abundance and become both His servant and slave. Hallelujah!

We are finally "FREED TO BE SERVANT AND SLAVE!"

Seven

Conclusion

This book imparts numerous positive and uplifting messages, including:

- Recognition of Tribulations: Understanding that tribulations are inherent in this fallen realm.
- Awareness of Cultural Dynamics: Awareness of the cultural "matrix" designed to enforce and entrench suffering, bondage, and oppression.
- Acknowledgment of Inescapable Enslavement: Knowledge that we are born into enslavement, making the crucial choice of deciding which master to be a slave to – satan or King Jesus/Yeshua.
- Revelation on Breaking Free: Insight on how to break free from the cultural matrix through the embrace of the yoke of Jesus.

- Repentance and Forgiveness as Mandates: Recognition that repentance and extending forgiveness are not optional but mandated by God.
- Contrast with Marxist Derivatives: Awareness that Critical Race Theory (CRT), Diversity, Equity, and Inclusion (DEI), Social Justice, Black Liberation Theology, and all Marxist derivatives are fundamentally antithetical to God's Word. They are designed to further tether humanity to the insidious cultural matrix.
- Debunking the "Sacred-Secular Divide": Dismissing the notion of a sacred-secular divide as a deception and self-serving excuse, emphasizing that it is a tool used to hinder Lordship.
- Consequences of Unforgiveness: Pointing out that church divisions, accusations, and condemnations confirm a lack of forgiveness. Those engaged in such mindsets face an existential crisis in their soul.
- Lordship in Decision-Making: Under Jesus' Lordship, even seemingly mundane acts like voting are not based solely on human emotion or tradition. Instead, our Master confirms our choices for His glory, emphasizing that decisions should not be left to emotions alone.

COSTLY DOWNSIDES

While this book offers valuable insights, there is a notable downside. Having delved into its contents, we are now unequivocally held accountable for our actions moving forward. The responsibility falls squarely on us, as God will hold us answerable for both our actions and inactions influenced by the knowledge gained from this read. Ignorance of insidious cultural trends and the significance of embracing the Lordship of Christ is no longer an excuse.

In essence, a crucial choice lies before us. The options are binary and diametrically opposed: (1) Persist in being a slave to satan and his dominion over our cultural matrix; or (2) Opt to choose God and His Kingdom authority by embracing the yoke of Jesus and submitting to His Lordship. The bottom line emphasizes the urgency of this decision and the transformative power it holds for our lives.

Simple....Choose wisely!

Endnotes

1. Gallup News, U.S Depression Rates Reach New highs, Dan Witters; Daily Signal, "..Suicide Rate Soars…, Nov 30,2023, Dan Hart
2. George Barna Millennial Report 2021
3. Leslie Fielder quoted in Trousered Apes, by Duncan Williams
4. The End of Christendom, Malcolm Muggeridge, Pg. 49

Acknowledgments

I extend my heartfelt appreciation to Mr. Terry Barnes for his exceptional contributions, particularly in the realm of cover designs. Terry deserves commendation for his unwavering dedication to his work, investing his God-given talents and skills with wholehearted commitment—a rare quality indeed. Consistently delivering remarkable Social Media and Graphic designs, Terry possesses the ability to transform modest ideas into true masterpieces. I am profoundly grateful for both his work and friendship.

Furthermore, the completion of this book benefitted significantly from the meticulous vetting and hermeneutic confirmation provided by Mr. Richard W. Stevens. In addition to being a valued friend, Mr. Stevens served as an editor and collaborator, bringing his profound intellect to the project. His thoughtful questions, depth of understanding on contemporary issues, and editorial prowess were instrumental in refining concepts and ideas, providing the necessary impetus and clarity for the successful completion of this endeavor.

Numerous friends have also generously provided their insights and perspectives in the development of this book. It stands as a culmination of theological excellence, a testament to the valuable input received from my networks of discipleship relationships and friend networks.

Additional resources:

Every Black Life Matters (EBLM) www.everyblm.com

- Follow us on all Social Media platforms
  - (YouTube/FB/Insta)
- Racial Unity and DEI Training and Consulting
- Racial Unity and DEI certification
- www.eblmrazist.net for additional information on confronting and combatting racism

"YallWOKEd Up University" on YouTube & Podcast- Check your favorite podcast providers

Other McGary books on **Amazon.com**:

- "DEI In 3D" *Deciphering Designs Demands and dilemmas of DEI*
- "**WOKEd Up!** *Finally Putting an Ax to the Taproot Of White Supremacy and racism in America"*
- "**The War On Women from The Root to The Fruit**... which side are you on?"
- "**Just Justly Justice!**"
- "**Instanity!**"

For Training and Speaking engagements, please contact: kevin@everyblm.com